U0751038

寰宇贸融

福费廷惯例3.9版

Universe Trade Finance Customs and
Practice for Forfaiting version 3.9

深圳市投友亲金融信息服务有限公司　著
Universe Trade Finance Information Service Co., Ltd.

厦门大学出版社　国家一级出版社
XIAMEN UNIVERSITY PRESS　全国百佳图书出版单位

图书在版编目(CIP)数据

寰宇贸融福费廷惯例 3.9 版＝Universe Trade Finance Customs and Practice for Forfaiting version 3.9 / 深圳市投友亲金融信息服务有限公司著.—厦门：厦门大学出版社，2018.12
ISBN 978-7-5615-7173-6

Ⅰ. ①寰…　Ⅱ. ①深…　Ⅲ. ①国际贸易—信用证　Ⅳ. ①F830.73

中国版本图书馆 CIP 数据核字(2018)第 247932 号

出 版 人	郑文礼
责任编辑	吴兴友
封面设计	夏 林
技术编辑	朱 楷

出版发行	厦门大学出版社
社　　址	厦门市软件园二期望海路 39 号
邮政编码	361008
总 编 办	0592-2182177　0592-2181406(传真)
营销中心	0592-2184458　0592-2181365
网　　址	http://www.xmupress.com
邮　　箱	xmupress@126.com
印　　刷	厦门集大印刷厂

开本	787 mm×1 092 mm　1/16
印张	5
字数	77 千字
版次	2018 年 12 月第 1 版
印次	2018 年 12 月第 1 次印刷
定价	30.00 元

本书如有印装质量问题请直接寄承印厂调换

厦门大学出版社
微信二维码

厦门大学出版社
微博二维码

序 言
FOREWORDS

Forfaiting 一词源自法语，是一种无追索权地贴现未到期债权的技术，在二战后由瑞士金融家为促进西德向东欧的固定资产出口贸易而开发，到20世纪90年代，福费廷已在全球市场上成为重要的贸易融资工具。

The word "Forfaiting" derived from French, it is a technique that discounting outstanding claims without recourse. Forfaiting was developed in the wake of World War II by Swiss financiers in order to facilitate the sale of West German capital assets to Eastern Europe.In the 1990s, forfaiting has become an important trade finance tool in the global market.

在中国，买断式贴现起源于唐代的汇票贴现，因此买断一词随汇票贴现自古流传至今。Forfaiting 业务在不同时期传入中国各地区后，部分地区音译为"福费廷"，部分地区意译为"买断"。主要用于信用证(信用状)项下的未到期债权买断。

In China, the discount without recourse originated from discounting bills of exchange in the Tang Dynasty. After the forfaiting business was introduced to different regions of China in different periods, in some regions it was transliterated as "forfaiting" and in some regions it was translated as "transfer without recourse". It is mainly used for the purchase of outstanding claims under the letter of credit.

鉴于福费廷业务在全球近70年发展已相当成熟，传入中国后又产生了诸多创新，业务模式和主要合同条款已在市场上形成惯例，因此我公司将现行的业务模式编写并出版为惯例的形式。

Our company has compiled and published the current business model in the form of

"Customs and Practice" in the view of the fact that forfaiting business has been matured over the past 70 years in the world, the business models and principal terms of the contract have formed a practice in forfaiting market, not to mention its innovations after the introduction to China.

国股大行的福费廷市场早已饱和，但中小银行国内证和出口信用证的发展还很不充分，其中交易对手不足导致交易渠道不畅是重大阻碍之一。

The forfaiting market of top tier banks has long been saturated. However, the domestic L/C and export L/C(may be issued by top tier banks) of small and medium-sized banks is still under development. One of the major obstacles is that the lack of counterparties leads to poor trading channels.

曾经，各家银行开办福费廷二级市场业务需要跟各家交易对手签署福费廷协议或法审电文文本才能开办业务，耗时费力。

In the past, any bank that wanted to starting a forfaiting secondary market transaction must sign forfaiting agreements or legal review SWIFT message text with its counterparties.

今后，各行只要与我公司签署《福费廷服务主合同》约定承认并接受该出版物，即有机会获得一批交易对手信息，有利于提高签约行的议价能力和询价视野，节省签约和法审的时间。

In the future, any bank that signs the *Master Forfaiting Service Contract* with our company and agreed to subject to the CPF(referred to the Licensed Bank hereafter), may obtain the information of counterparties, which is helpful to improve the bargain capacity of the Licensed bank and increase the inquiry options, saving time for both signing and legal reviewing.

签约行间可通过在电文或文件中声明遵循惯例办理福费廷业务，其原理如同信用证对 UCP 的引用。业务模式如下图：

Licensed banks may make forfaiting transaction that expressly indicates to subject to the CPF in Transaction Document and the principle is the same as L/C reference to UCP. The CPF business mode is illustrated as follows:

交易流程/Procedure for forfaiting transaction

本公司（信息服务商）
Our company
(Grantor)

已签主合同
Signed contract

已签主合同
Signed contract

流程步骤/Procedure

签约行A（出证）
Bank A
(Grantor)

发福费廷申请书（惯例附件1）
Cend Offer Letter (Appendix 1)

回福费廷确认函（惯例附件2）
return Confirmation of Offer
Letter (Appendix 2)

发债权转让书（惯例附件3）
Send Letter of Assignment (Appendix 2)

签约行B（收证）
Bank B
(Purchaser)

发债权转让通知（惯例附件4）
Send Notice of Assignment (Appendix 2)

债务人/承兑行
Obligor/Accept-
ing Bank

放款/Payment

虽然，签约行之间没有签字盖章形式的签约，但是每一份引用惯例的要约或电文都是买卖双方自主签订的业务合同，具有法律效力。

Although there is no signed or sealed contract form between the Licensed Banks, each offer letter/message that expressly indicates to subject to the CPF will be treated as a business contract signed independently by the Grantor Bank and the Purchaser Bank, which has legal effect.

通过 SWIFT、区块链信用证系统或者人行大额支付系统发出的电文，比签字盖章的纸质文件更难抵赖或伪造，安全性更高。出版物公开发行后有公开性和不可修改性，电文或文件中对出版物 ISBN 编号的引用将确保交易遵循唯一且一致的法律文本。

The message via SWIFT, block chain based L/C system or HVPS is harder to be denied or forged than the paper documents signed and sealed, and the security is higher. The CPF is published with publicness, uniqueness and Non-Modifiability. The ISBN number expressly referred in transaction message or documents will ensure the transaction is subject to the unique and same legal text.

本惯例支持海外法人银行要求以英文为准适用英国法或其所在地法律，支持没有 SWIFT 的城商农商通过人行大额支付系统发送电文。人行大额支付系统的自由格式电文

不得超过127个汉字或255字符，本惯例所设计的电文模板可满足其字数要求。人行大额支付系统电文可直接对接中国大陆任何一家银行，不仅安全高效而且无需额外开发系统，能节约签约行的科技成本。

The CPF can meet the need of the overseas banks using English in transactions with the governing law of their homelands or England. And the transactions between city commercial banks and rural commercial banks that send message via HVPS if those bank have no SWIFT can also be supported. The free format message of HVPS must not exceed 255 English bytes. The message template in CPF can satisfy the word count requirement thereof. The HVPS message can directly connect to any bank in mainland China. It is not only safe and efficient, but also does not need to develop other systems, which can save the technology cost of the Licensed bank.

如今，全球已有许多区块链信用证系统或区块链贸易融资系统，互联互通还很困难。我公司为未来可能遇到的区块链系统考虑，为支持自由格式电文和信用证产品的区块链系统预留了可用的电文格式，期待免建押的系统能有全球互通的一天。

Nowadays, there are many block chain based L/C Systems or block chain based trade finance Systems all over the world, and they are still difficult to interconnect. For any block chain system that may be encountered in the future, our company has reserved some message format for the block chain system that support free format message and L/C. Our company look forward to a day of global interconnections for block chain based L/C system.

虽然各行现行模式和单据要求各有不同，但是在惯例的电文或文件中已根据求同存异的原则预留了各类模式的选项。

Various options have been reserved in the messages or documents that are in appendix of the CPF according to the principle of seeking common ground while reserving differences and since the business mode and documents requirement varies in different banks.

买卖双方可在协商一致的前提下勾选有关选项或增补有关单据要求。

The Grantor Bank and the Purchaser Bank may choose the relevant options or supplementary terms under the premise of consensus.

根据主合同和惯例的约定，我公司作为信息中介协助买卖双方达成初步业务合作意向。我公司不做买卖双方的交易对手，不得为任何福费廷业务提供担保。

The Grantor Bank and the Purchaser Bank enter into the procedure for quotations and offers with the introduction of our company.And our company act as information broker. Our company shall not be counterparty of the Grantor Bank or the Purchaser Bank and willl not guarantee for any forfaiting transactions.

我公司将提供电文半自动生成工具，提高经办行工作效率，减少填写差错。通过我公司的询报价服务可节约寻找交易对手的时间。通过本惯例，建设包括中资银行和海外银行在内的信用证流通网络。

Our company shall provide semi-automatic generation tools for SWIFT/HVPS/block chain messages to improve licensed banks work efficiency and reduce inputting mistakes.Our inquiry service may save your time in finding counterparties.Our company will build a circulation network of L/C from Chinese banks and overseas banks by the CPF.

本惯例虽然预留了收费条款，但并不意味着我公司将唯利是图，雁过拔毛。对于难度较高，较为复杂的业务，我公司在与买卖双方协商一致的前提下可能会收取部分费用，但就目前开展的业务而言，大部分并不收费，难以付费的银行也不必担心，在时机合适时同样可使用本惯例。

Although the CPF reserves the terms of broker fee, it does not mean that our company will be seeking nothing but profits and charge for every transaction. Our company may charge those difficult and complex transactions with the prior consent of the Grantor Bank and the Purchaser Bank. But not for the most of the current business.If your bank is hard to pay for any fee,the CPF may be used when the time is right without any charge,so that you do not need to worry about it.

虽然我公司立足于中国市场，但这份惯例可用于面向全球的福费廷交易，并不局限

![Universe Trade Finance logo] 深圳市投友亲金融信息服务有限公司
Universe Trade Finance Information Service Co., Ltd.
网站/Website:www.forfaiting.ltd; www.forfaiting.shop

于单一的国家或地区。

Although our company is based on the Chinese market, the CPF can be used for forfaiting transactions around the world, not limited to a single country or region.

在编写过程中给予指导和支持的银行专家和律师，已列于本书编写顾问组，我公司向各位顾问诚致谢意。我公司将全力支持各家签约行的业务发展，携手共赢。

Our company would like to thank for bank experts and lawyers who provide guidance and support during the course of the CPF drafting. They are listed in the consultative group of this book. Our Company will fully support the business development of each licensed bank, to achieve the goal of and win-win.

史翔 /Shi Xiang

深圳市投友亲金融信息服务有限公司总经理

General manager,Universe Trade Finance Information Service Co., Ltd.

2018-10-15

深圳市投友亲金融信息服务有限公司
Universe Trade Finance Information Service Co., Ltd.
网站 /Website:www.forfaiting.ltd; www.forfaiting.shop

目 录

CONTENTS

深圳市投友亲金融信息服务有限公司
Universe Trade Finance Information Service Co., Ltd.
网站 /Website:www.forfaiting.ltd; www.forfaiting.shop

正文（用于签约行间福费廷业务)/Body Text

寰宇贸融福费廷惯例3.9版

Universe Trade Finance Customs and Practice for Forfaiting version 3.9

本出版物《寰宇贸融福费廷惯例3.9版》[ISBN:978-7-5615-7173-6](以下简称 "本惯例"）由深圳市投友亲金融信息服务有限公司 (以下简称 "发起人"）编著 , 作为交易规则用于签约行间明示遵循本惯例的福费廷业务。买卖双方根据交易地位互称为 "卖出行" 和 "买入行"。

This publication *Universe Trade Finance Customs and Practice for Forfaiting version 3.9*(ISBN: 978-7-5615-7173-6, hereinafter called "the CPF") is compiled by Universe Trade Finance Information Service Co., Ltd.(hereinafter called "Originator"),and acts as the trading rules for forfaiting transactions between Licensed Banks that expressly indicate subject to the "CPF" .Trading parties each hereinafter the "Grantor Bank" and the "Purchaser Bank" as the case may be.

一、释义

Article 1. Definitions

1.1**寰宇贸融**，指发起人贸易融资业务品牌。

Universe Trade Finance means a brand of trade financing business owned by the Originator.

1.2**福费廷业务**，指卖出行作为贸易融资项下未到期债权未到期债权（以下简称 "相关债权"）的唯一合法受益人或其代理人，在相关债权已由买入行认可的银行出具 / 加具了真实有效的承兑 / 保兑的情况下，将其按约定的交易价格全部或部分无追索权地转让给买入行的业务。

Forfaiting transaction means the transaction that the Grantor Bank acts as the sole legal and beneficial owner or owner's broker of outstanding payment claim(hereinafter "relevant claim") under trade finance, Where the relevant claim has been issued/confirmed by a bank approved by the Purchaser Bank, should be transferred wholly or partially to the Purchaser Bank without recourse at the agreed transaction price.

1.3 **签约行**，指与发起人签约《福费廷服务主合同》且约定遵循本惯例的银行。

Licensed Bank means any bank that signs the *Master Forfaiting Service Contract* with the originator and agree to subject to the CPF.

1.4 **交易文件**，指在福费廷交易中的所涉及的文件和电文，包括但不限于明确引用本惯例的文件或电文，《福费廷申请书》（格式见附件1）、《债权转让书》（格式见附件3）、通过大额支付系统发送的债权转让确认电文（格式见附件7）等。

Transaction Document(s) means any document or message via SWIFT/HVPS/block chain system in a forfaiting transaction, including but not limited to any forfaiting transaction that expressly referred to the CPF, *Offer Letter*(substantially in the form as set out in Appendix 1 hereof),*Letter of Assignment*(substantially in the form as set out in Appendix 3 hereof), *Confirmation of Letter of Assignment via HVPS*(substantially in the form as set out in Appendix 7 hereof),*etc*.

1.5 **买卖双方**，指福费廷业务中的买入行和卖出行。

Trading parties means the Grantor Bank and the Purchaser Bank in forfaiting transaction.

1.6 **债务人**，指向因商品或服务交易产生的未到期债权做出承兑、保兑的金融机构。

Obligor means Financial Institution that has an obligation under acceptance/confirmation for outstanding claims based on goods or services trade.

1.7 **贴现率**，指商定的综合利率或 LIBOR 加点。

Discount rate means the agreed All-in rate or margin (reflecting the risk of the Obligor & the country exposure) plus LIBOR.

1.8 **贴现期**，即融资天数，指买入行向卖出行付款起息日至相关债权到期日之间的实际天数加宽限期（如有），根据支付的币种的差异，一年以360天或365天计算。（支付的货币币种为英镑、港币、新加坡元、马来西亚林吉特的，一年为365天，支付其他币种的一年均为360天）

Discounting period means the actual number of days between the value date and the maturity date of the relevant claims plus grace period (if any) based on a 360 or 365 days a year. (365 days a year just for currencies like British Pounds, Hong Kong Dollars, Singapore Dollars, Malaysian Ringgits respectively or such currency as may be agreed by the Grantor Bank and the Purchaser Bank from time to time)

1.9 **LIBOR**，指伦敦银行间同业市场拆借利率，其取值为福费廷交易的计息日前两

个工作日由伦敦洲际交易所 (ICE) 旗下洲际交易所基准管理机构 (IBA) 在伦敦时间上午 11:00 公布的相关货币和期限的利率，可通过路透社或彭博社相关页面查询。如果路透社或彭博社页面没有该利率或必须确定当前时间之后的利率，以伦敦银行间同业市场主流银行该币种可比金额向出借人提供存放的年利率确定，如利率低于0，则 LIBOR 应确定为0。

LIBOR means, for any amount and any period, the London interbank offered rate (as administered by the Intercontinental Exchange Benchmark Administration Limited or any successor administrator of that rate) for the relevant currency and that period (or the nearest period either side of that period for which a rate is published, interpolated as necessary in accordance with the Lender's standard practice), as displayed on the applicable Reuters or Bloomberg screen (or any other rate display service acceptable to the Parties), at or about 11.00 a.m. London time two Business Days before the start of that period or, if no such interest rate appears on the selected display service or if the rate must be determined after that time, the rate per annum at which the Lender was offered deposits in that currency and a comparable amount by leading banks in the London interbank market for that period at or about the time at which the rate is required to be determined and if the rate is less than zero, LIBOR shall be determined to be zero.

1.10 **ISBN**，指国际标准书号。

ISBN means The International Standard Book Number

1.11 **人行**，指中国人民银行。

PBOC means The People's Bank Of China.

1.12 **ICC**，指国际商会

ICC means the International Chamber of Commerce

1.13 **CIPS**，指中国人民银行的人民币跨境支付系统

CIPS means The Cross-border Interbank Payment System Produced by PBOC

1.14 **人行支付系统**，指中国人民银行的中国国家现代化支付系统。

CNAPS means The China National Advanced Payment System Produced by PBOC.

1.15 **大额支付系统**，指中国人民银行的大额实时支付子系统。

HVPS means The High Value Payment System Produced by PBOC.

1.16 **关联公司**，指直接或间接控制或受控于该方或者与该方受到共同直接或间接控

制的公司或其他实体

Affiliates means corporation(s) or other entity(entities) that directly or indirectly take control of the other or is directly/indirectly controlled by or under common Control as, such Party.

1.17 **专业顾问**，指由一方为福费廷业务而雇用的负责提供建议的律师、会计师、审计师、财务顾问、银行和其他专业或技术顾问及其承包人；

Professional Advisors means lawyers, accountants, auditors, financial advisers, bankers and other professionals or technical advisers and their employees and contractors retained by either Party providing professional suggestions for the forfaiting transaction.

1.18 **工作日**，指买卖双方所在国家或地区银行正常营业的一天。如果相关交易的支付货币与前述国家或地区的货币不同，则"工作日"也应包括支付货币所在地金融中心的银行正常营业的一天。

Business day means a day (not being a Saturday or Sunday) on which banks are open for business in the jurisdictions of both the Grantor Bank and the Purchaser Bank, and if the currency of payment concerning the relevant Transaction is different from the currency in the aforesaid jurisdictions, also means a day on which banks are open for business in the financial center of the currency of that relevant transaction.

二、总则
Article 2. General Provisions

2.1 惯例效力：

Effectiveness of the CPF:

签约行之间在交易文件中声明遵循本惯例的，该交易文件属于买卖双方自由缔约的独立业务合同，本惯例是该业务合同不可分割的一部分。发起人作为信息中介，不做买卖双方的交易对手，不经手任何交易单据。发起人为买卖双方提供询报价、业务信息咨询，发起人可在买卖双方同意的情况下，就单笔业务收取金融信息服务费。

如交易文件中未声明引用本惯例，可适用买卖双方另行签订的有关福费廷协议。

Any transaction document(s) made between Licensed Banks that expressly claim subject to the CPF, attribute(s) to an independent business contract signed between the Grantor Bank and the Purchaser Bank on their free will with the CPF being an integral part of it.The Originator, as information broker, shall not act as counterparty in transaction between the Grantor Bank and the

Purchaser Bank,shall not handle any transaction document. The Originator shall not guarantee for any forfaiting transaction. The services that the Originator provide to Trading parties includes price inquiry, transaction information consultation likewise. The Originator may charge Trading parties for broker service fee by transaction with the prior consent of Trading parties.

In case when transaction document does not declare reference to the CPF,this transaction shall be governed by any forfaiting agreement signed by both the Grantor Bank and the Purchaser Bank.

2.2福费廷服务主合同法律效力：

Effectiveness of the *Master Forfaiting Service Contract*：

本惯例是《福费廷服务主合同》的附件，遵循本惯例的签约行必须与发起人签订并遵循《福费廷服务主合同》。如果本惯例与《福费廷服务主合同》出现任何不一致，以**本惯例**的规定为准，除非买卖双方和发起人另有书面约定。

Since the CPF acts as an Appendix to the *Master Forfaiting Service Contract*, the licensed bank that subject to the CPF, must be the one that signed the *Master Forfaiting Service Contract* with the Originator. It is the CPF that prevails, in case of inconsistency existed between the *Master Forfaiting Service Contract* and the CPF, unless the trading parties and the Originator expressly otherwise agreed in writing.

2.3交易文件法律效力：

Effectiveness of the Transaction Document(s):

买卖双方进行每次福费廷交易时需签署交易文件，本惯例中的条款和条件同样适用于每一份交易文件，每一份交易文件和本惯例应视为同一个整体予以理解和解释。 如果《福费廷服务主合同》或本惯例与**交易文件**出现任何不一致，以**交易文件**的规定为准，买卖双方另有书面约定的除外。

Under each Forfaiting Transaction from time to time, the Transaction Document(s) will be necessary, the terms and conditions of the CPF shall be i_____ into each Transaction Document which shall be read and construed as w_____ of any inconsistency between the *Master Forfaiting Service* _____ ransaction Document(s),it is the Transaction Document(s) that shall _____ essly agreed otherwise in writing by Trading parties.

5

三、福费廷交易规则及流程

Article 3. Rule and Procedure for Forfaiting Transaction

3.1. **交易条件：**

Operation Conditions:

买卖双方及发起人同意每笔福费廷交易遵守下列条款，另有书面约定的除外：

Trading parties and Originator agree that, unless otherwise agreed in writing, any forfaiting transaction shall be binding on the following terms:

3.1.1 债务人已对福费廷交易标的：债权工具或应收账款做出承兑或保证付款。

The instruments/receivables the subject of the Forfaiting Purchase have been accepted or confirmed to pay by the relevant Obligor.

3.1.2 买入行没有对相关债权项下已提交的单据进行审核的义务。

The Purchaser Bank has no obligation to examine the documents presented under relevant claim.

3.1.3 国际信用证业务应遵循国际商会《跟单信用证统一惯例（UCP600）》或其此后更新版本的相关规定。国内信用证业务依据中国人民银行颁布的国内信用证的现行有效管理规定办理。

The Import L/C is subject to ICC UCP 600 version or any subsequent revision as may be adopted by ICC. The Domestic L/C is subject to the rules on Domestic Letter of Credit published by PBOC.

3.1.4 相关债权项下的条款和条件对于买入行是可接受的。

The terms and conditions of relevant claim are acceptable to the Purchaser Bank.

3.1.5 福费廷交易相关债权的债务人及相关债权所涉国家或地区对于买入行是可接受的。

The Obligor and the country or jurisdiction of relevant claim are acceptable to the Purchaser Bank.

3.1.6 买卖双方根据发起人提供的信息达成初步意向进入要约阶段。经买卖双方同意，发起人可向买入行或卖出行收取金融信息服务费，发起人向付费方开具发票（如有）。

With the introduction of Originator, the Grantor Bank and the Purchaser Bank enter the offer stage with preliminary consensus.The Originator may charge the Grantor Bank or the Purchaser Bank for broker service fee with the prior consent of Trading parties. The Originator

shall issue invoices (if any)to the payer.

3.1.7 买卖双方遵循本惯例第三章（福费廷交易规则及流程）之规定完成交易。

The Grantor Bank and the Purchaser Bank shall complete the transaction subject to Article 3

3.2 **交易文件传递方式**：

Transaction document delivery:

买卖双方经协商一致，买卖双方有权选择 SWIFT、支持自由格式电文的区块链信用证系统或邮寄配合大额支付系统确认电文三种方式传递交易文件。

Trading parties may deliver Transaction Document(s) via SWIFT, block chain based L/C system that supporting free format message or post with confirmation message via HVPS.

3.2.1 选择 SWIFT 系统的：买卖双方应先行建立密押关系，通过加押电文通讯。

Deliver Transaction Document(s) via SWIFT: Trading parties must establish relationship in RMA (Relationship Management Application in SWIFT) before they deliver messages via authenticated SWIFT.

3.2.2 选择邮寄配合大额支付系统确认电的：买卖双方可选择通过预留印鉴及签字样本（格式见附件9，或自有印鉴片）或大额支付系统确认电文（在电文中声明签章真实）验证交易文件的真实性。经交易双方协商一致，可先采用传真或 Email 发送交易文件的传真件或扫描件，传真件或扫描件上的签章具有法律效力。发件人应在传真或 Email 发出后立即将纸质原件邮寄给对方。

Transaction Document(s) delivery via post with Confirmation message via HVPS: Trading parties shall verify the authenticity of the transaction documents by the *reserved seal(if any) and signature sample* (substantially in the form as set out in Appendix 9 hereof or other facsimiles between Trading parties) or confirmation message[expressly indicate chop/seal(s) and/or signature(s) are authentic] via HVPS. Trading parties may send Scanning copies of Transaction Document(s) via fax/e-mail with the prior consent of Trading parties, The signature and seal on the scanned copies of Transaction Document(s) are legally valid. The Original Paper Document(s) must be sent to other party by post without delay in time when the scanning copies of the transaction document(s) has been sent out.

3.2.3 选择通过区块链信用证系统的：如买卖双方已建有可互联互通且支持自由格式电文的区块链信用证系统的，可通过该系统发送电文。

Deliver Transaction Document(s) via block chain based L/C system: Trading parties may

send messages via block chain system, after they have built a block chain based L/C system that can interconnect and support free format messages.

3.3 交易流程：

Procedure for forfaiting transaction:

3.3.1 要约

Procedure for Quotations and Offers:

叙做每笔福费廷业务时卖出行需签发《福费廷申请书》(格式见附件1)，买入行需签发《福费廷确认函》(格式见附件2)。买卖双方应根据遵循本惯例3.3.1.1或3.3.1.2条款的规定完成要约流程。

Under the forfaiting transaction from time to time, an *Offer Letter* (substantially in the form as set out in Appendix 1 hereof) issued by the Grantor Bank and a *Forfaiting Confirmation* (substantially in the form as set out in Appendix 2 hereof) issued by the Purchaser Bank will be necessary. Trading parties shall agree to be binding by Clause 3.3.1.1 or Clause 3.3.1.2 for completing this procedure.

3.3.1.1 通过 SWIFT 或区块链信用证系统电文办理：

Transaction via SWIFT or block chain based L/C system:

(1) 对于本惯例下每笔福费廷业务，卖出行通过 SWIFT 或区块链信用证系统向买入**行发送《福费廷申请书》**(格式见附件1)提出要约。

For each Forfaiting transaction that subject to the CPF from time to time, the Grantor Bank shall send *Offer Letter* (substantially in the form as set out in Appendix 1 hereof) which act as request for quotation to the Purchaser Bank via SWIFT or block chain based L/C system.

(2) 买入行收到卖出行的《福费廷申请书》后，有权自行决定受理与否。若买入行同意受理的，应在《福费廷申请书》约定的截止期限内通过 SWIFT 或区块链信用证系统向卖出行回复《福费廷确认函》(格式见附件2)确认接受该笔交易。

Once the Purchaser Bank receives the Offer Letter that issued by the Grantor Bank via SWIFT, the Purchaser Bank may send *Forfaiting Confirmation*(substantially in the form as set out in Appendix 2 hereof) which acting as confirming offer within the deadline of this Offer Letter to the Grantor Bank via SWIFT or block chain based L/C system.

3.3.1.2 邮寄文件配合大额支付系统确认电文办理：

Transaction Document(s) sent by post should be processed with Confirmation message via

HVPS

(1) 对于本惯例下每笔福费廷业务，卖出行根据本惯例3.2.2条款规定的方式签发《福费廷申请书》(格式见附件1) 向买入行提出要约，卖出行可选择通过大额支付系统向买入行发送确认电文予以确认 (格式见附件5)。

For each Forfaiting transaction that subject to the CPF, the Grantor Bank shall issue *Offer Letter* (substantially in the form as set out in Appendix 1 hereof)which act as request for quotation to the Purchaser Bank subject to Clause 3.2.2, and the Grantor Bank may choose to send Confirmation message(substantially in the form as set out in Appendix 5 hereof) to the Purchaser Bank via HVPS.

(2) 买入行根据本惯例3.2.2条款规定的方式收到卖出行《福费廷申请书》后，有权自行决定受理与否。若买入行同意受理的，应在《福费廷申请书》约定的截止期限内根据本惯例3.2.2条款规定的方式向卖出行回复《福费廷确认函》(格式见附件2) 确认接受该笔交易。买入行可选择通过大额支付系统向卖出行发送确认电文予以确认 (格式见附件6)

Once the Purchaser Bank receives the *Offer Letter* issued by the Grantor Bank that subject to Clause 3.2.2, the Purchaser Bank may send *Forfaiting Confirmation*(substantially in the form as set out in Appendix 2 hereof) which acting as confirming offer within the deadline of this *Offer Letter* to the Grantor Bank subject to Clause 3.2.2, and The Purchaser Bank may choose to send *Confirmation of Forfaiting Confirmation*(substantially in the form as set out in Appendix 6 hereof) to the Grantor Bank via HVPS.

3.3.1.3交易双方应在《福费廷申请书》及《福费廷确认函》中明示对该笔业务有效的联系方式。

Trading parties must expressly indicate their effective contact details for this transaction in *Offer Letter* and *Forfaiting Confirmation*.

3.3.2债权转让 :

Procedure for assignment:

交易双方完成要约后，卖出行应在《福费廷申请书》规定的时间内完成债权转让。交易双方应根据本惯例3.3.2.1或3.3.2.2条款规定的流程发送《债权转让书》。

After the procedure for Quotations and Offers, the Grantor Bank must complete this procedure within the deadline of this *Offer Letter*. Trading parties shall abide by Clause 3.3.2.1 or Clause 3.3.2.2 for completing of this procedure.

9

3.3.2.1通过 SWIFT 或区块链信用证系统办理：

Via SWIFT or block chain based L/C system:

卖出行根据《福费廷申请书》约定的条件，通过 SWIFT 加押电文或区块链信用证系统电文向买入行发送《债权转让书》(格式见附件3)。

According to the terms and conditions of *Offer Letter*, the Grantor Bank shall send *Letter of Assignment*(substantially in the form as set out in Appendix 3 hereof) to the Purchaser Bank via authenticated SWIFT or block chain based L/C system.

3.3.2.2邮寄文件配合大额支付系统确认电办理。

Transaction Document(s) sent by post should be processed with Confirmation message via HVPS:

卖出行根据《福费廷申请书》约定的条件，按照本惯例3.2.2条款规定的方式向买入行发出《债权转让书》(格式见附件3)，卖出行必须通过大额支付系统向买入行发送确认电文予以确认(格式见附件7)。

According to the terms and conditions of *Offer Letter*, The Grantor Bank shall send *Letter of Assignment*(substantially in the form as set out in Appendix 3 hereof) to the Purchaser Bank abide by Clause 3.2.2.And the Grantor Bank must send *Confirmation of Letter of Assignment* to the Purchaser Bank via HVPS(substantially in the form as set out in Appendix 7 hereof)

3.3.3通知债务人债权转让事宜：

Procedure for notifying to the Obligor of the assignment:

当卖出行不是债务人时，卖出行应发送《转让通知书》(格式见附件4)通知债务人信用证项下相关权利和收益已被无条件不可撤销地让渡给"买入行"，同时要求对此通知予以回复确认。交易双方应选择本惯例3.3.3.1或3.3.3.2条款规定的流程通知债务人。

In case when the Grantor Bank is not the Obligor, the Grantor Bank shall send *Notice of Assignment* (substantially in the form as set out in Appendix 4 hereof) to the Obligor advising that the rights and proceeds of the L/C have been irrevocably and unconditionally assigned to the Purchaser Bank, and requesting a reply and comfirmation of notice.Trading parties shall abide by Clause 3.3.3.1 or Clause 3.3.3.2 for completing this procedure.

3.3.3.1通过 SWIFT 或区块链信用证系统办理。卖出行通过 SWIFT 加押电文或区块链信用证系统电文向债务人发送《转让通知书》(格式见附件4)。

Via SWIFT or block chain based L/C system: The Grantor Bank should send *Notice*

of Assignment (substantially in the form as set out in Appendix 4 hereof) to Obligor via authenticated SWIFT or block chain based L/C system.

3.3.3.2邮寄文件配合大额支付系统确认电办理。卖出行应根据本惯例3.2.2条款规定的方式向债务人发送《转让通知书》(格式见附件4) 并通过大额支付系统向债务人发送转让通知电文 (格式见附件8)。

Transaction Document(s) send by post should be processed with Confirmation message via HVPS: The Grantor Bank should send *Notice of Assignment* (substantially in the form as set out in Appendix 4 hereof) to the Obligor under Clause 3.2.2. Once the *Notice of Assignment* has been sent, the Grantor Bank shall send *Confirmation of Notice of Assignment*(substantially in the form as set out in Appendix 8 hereof) to the Obligor via HVPS without delay.

3.3.4单据递送：

Documentation delivery:

3.3.4.1卖出行根据《福费廷确认函》中的联系方式和《福费廷申请书》约定的条件向买入行提供单据，有关单据应符合本惯例3.3.4.2之要求。

The Grantor Bank shall deliver documentation(s) to the Purchaser Bank abiding by the contact details of *Forfaiting Confirmation* and the terms and conditions of *Offer Letter*, The documentation(s) shall be subject to Clause 3.3.4.2.

3.3.4.2 单据要求：

Documentations required:

根据本惯例第3.4.1条，卖出行应向买入行提供下列单据：

Under Clause 3.4.1, the following documentationsis required to be provided from the Grantor Bank to the Purchaser Bank:

(1) 经卖出行证实的相关债权文件（例如：信用证）及所有修改（如有）的真实有效复印件；

Certified true copy of relevant claim(e.g.L/C) and all amendments thereto;

(2) 经卖出行证实的债务人以 SWIFT 加押电文、区块链信用证系统、中国人民银行大额支付系统发出的承兑电或纸质付款确认书的真实有效复印件，承兑内容包括确认债务人接受单据及付款到期日 , 并保证在到期日付款；

Certified true copy of the acceptance notice in authenticated SWIFT format, block chain based L/C system, HVPS or paper documentation from the Obligor to the Grantor Bank

confirming its acceptance of documents and maturity dates and that, at maturity date the funds will be remitted to the Grantor Bank according to its instruction;

（3）卖出行通过 SWIFT 加押授权电文、区块链信用证系统电文或中国人民银行大额支付系统电文确认发送给买入行的《债权转让书》（格式见附件3），声明将相关债权下所有权利和收益转让给买入行；

Duly executed *Letter of Assignment* (substantially in the form as set out in Appendix 3 hereof) via authenticated SWIFT, block chain based L/C system or HVPS Confirmation from the Grantor Bank to the Purchaser Bank assigning all benefits of the payment under relevant claim to the Purchaser Bank.

（4）经卖出行证实的卖出行通过 SWIFT 加押电文、区块链电文或中国人民银行大额支付系统电文确认发送给债务人的《转让通知书》的真实有效复印件（格式见附件4、附件8）；

Certified true copy of the Notice of Assignment(substantially in the form as set out in Appendix 4 hereof) by authenticated SWIFT, block chain message or HVPS Confirmation(substantially in the form as set out in Appendix 8 hereof) from the Grantor Bank to the Obligor;

（5）经买卖双方一致同意，买入行要求的其他单据，由卖出行在《福费廷申请书》中载明。

With the prior consent of Trading parties, the Grantor Bank may expressly indicate in *Offer Letter* when other documentations are requested by the Purchaser Bank .

3.4 付款

Payment：

3.4.1买入行的付款条件为：

The conditions of payment for the Purchaser Bank are as follows:

3.4.1.1买入行已收到形式和内容均符合其要求的单据（定义于本惯例第3.3.4.2条）；

The Purchaser Bank has received the Documentation (as described in Clause 3.3.4.2 of the CPF) in satisfied form and substance;

3.4.1.2交易文件及本惯例下的各项条款和条件均已履行；

All terms and conditions of the Transaction Document(s) and the CPF have been fulfilled;

3.4.1.3卖出行将相关债权下的全部权益已合法有效地转让给买入行；

All the rights and benefits under the relevant claim have been legally and validly assigned by the Grantor Bank to the Purchaser Bank;

3.4.1.4 卖出行已将转让事宜通知债务人。

The Assignment has been notified to the Obligor.

3.4.2 买入行向卖出行付款：

Payment by the Purchaser Bank to the Grantor Bank:

3.4.2.1 在本惯例 3.4.1 条件的全部履行后，买入行应在收到卖出行提供的符合要求的单据（见本惯例第 3.3.4.2 条）后 2 个工作日内向卖出行付款，付款金额为应收账款总金额及 / 或应收账款面值中扣除双方商定的费用及利息后得到净值。

When the terms in Clause 3.4.1 has fully completed, the Purchaser Bank shall pay the Grantor Bank within 2 Business Days (as defined hereinafter) after reception of the Documentation (as described in Clause 3.3.4.2) in form and substance satisfactory to it. The net proceeds should be the net amount payable by the Purchaser Bank to the Grantor Bank after deducting the fees, (commission and interests included) in respect of the Forfaiting Purchase calculated in accordance with Clause 4 from the gross amounts of the instruments and/or face value of the receivables under the Rrelevant claim.

3.4.2.2 交易双方在福费廷交易中的所有付款应按照交易文件及本惯例的相关规定，以立即可使用的、可自由划转的资金支付给对方，所支付款项不能有任何抵消或反诉，以及因税费产生的任何抵扣或预提。如因税费而产生了任何扣减或预提，支付方应将该税费支付给对方，以保证对方收到其应该收到的金额。所有付款应支付到交易文件所列明的账户。

All payments under the Forfaiting Transaction shall be made in accordance with each Transaction Document(s) and the CPF in immediately available and freely transferable funds without set off or counter-claim and free of any deduction or withholding for or on account of any tax, levy and charges whatsoever. In the event that any deduction or withholding for or on account of tax, levy and charge is required to be made, the paying party shall pay such additional amounts as to ensure that the receiving party receives and retains the amount it would have received. All payments shall be made to the account specified by each party to the other in accordance with the Transaction Document(s).

3.4.2.3 交易文件中有明确约定金融信息服务费及付款路径的，付款方应同时向发起人

支付费用。

In cases that broker service fees and Payment Methods are expressly indicated in Transaction Document(s), the fees shall be paid to the Originator from payer without delay.

3.4.3 如卖出行未及时向买入行支付本惯例第3.5.2（4）条和第3.5.3（2）条规定的款项，买入行有权自款项应付未付之日起至实际收到款项之日为止，按交易文件约定的**贴现率加1**% 向卖出行按日计收罚息。

In cases that the Grantor Bank fails to pay the payments under Clause 3.5.2(4) and Clause 3.5.3(2) in time, the Purchaser Bank may charge additional daily penalty with interests be calculated at the discount rate that expressly indicated in Transaction Document(s) plus 1% per day.

3.5. 双方的声明、保证及责任：

Representations, Warranties and Responsibilities:

3.5.1 卖出行及买入行相互声明并保证：

The Grantor Bank and the Purchaser Bank represents and warrants to each other that:

(1) 买卖双方有权发送、签订、执行本惯例及有关交易文件，并已获得必要的授权以履行本惯例及有关交易文件下的权利和义务。双方在所有文件上的签章或密押均真实有效，具有法律效力。

Trading parties has full power and authority to enter into and has duly authorized the execution and delivery of the CPF, each Transaction Document(s) and has obtained proper consents needed consents to exercise its rights and perform its obligations under the CPF and each Transaction Document(s). Trading parties' signature or RMA(Relationship Management Application in SWIFT) on all documents are authentic and effective, with legal effect.

(2) 买卖双方在本惯例及有关交易文件中的责任义务是合法、有效、有约束力，并根据相关条款和条件可执行的义务。

All the obligations of Trading parties under the CPF together with the relevant Transaction Document(s) are legal, valid and binding on Trading parties, and all the obligations are executable accordance with its terms and conditions.

3.5.2 卖出行进一步声明并保证：

The Grantor Bank further acknowledges and agrees that:

(1) 卖出行拥有的未到期相关债权是合法的，且此债权不受任何第三方的留置、限制、

抵销、反索偿、股权或优先求偿权所干涉。

To the best of the knowledge and belief of the Grantor Bank as at the date of the relevant Forfaiting Transaction, the documentation, instruments and/or receivables, which are the subject of the Forfaiting Transaction, are legal and free from all liens, charges or other encumbrances.

(2) 卖出行的债权真实有效、不可抗辩并且可自由转让。

The Grantor Bank's obligatory rights are real, effective, incontestable and freely transferable.

(3) 卖出行不会采取影响相关债权有效性或影响债务人发出的承兑有效性的不当行动。

The Grantor Bank will not take any actions that might affect the validity of relevant claim or of the acceptance to be given by the Obligor.

(4) 对于已经根据本惯例办理转让的款项，如果债务人将相关债权项下的相关款项仍支付给卖出行而未支付给买入行，卖出行保证在收到债务人所付款项后立即将收到的全部款项支付给买入行。

On maturity, if payment under a relevant claim is made to the Grantor Bank instead of the Purchaser Bank, the Grantor Bank undertakes that it will transfer the funds received under relevant claim to the account of the Purchaser Bank upon receipt of the same without delay.

(5) 如债务人违约，卖出行在由买入行承担相关费用和风险的前提下，将根据买入行的要求为其提供一切合理的帮助来追偿欠款。

In the event of an Obligor's default under the terms of a relevant claim, the Grantor Bank will grant all reasonable assistance at the request of the Purchaser Bank to recover the proceeds at the expense of the Purchaser Bank.

(6) 根据本惯例第3.4条关于债权合法有效转让的规定，卖出行不得在未经买入行事前同意的情况下，认同债务人的作为或不作为、行使或放弃行使卖出行在相关交易或单据下应有的权利或救济。

Subject to any relevant Assignment being legally and validly been executed in accordance with Clause 3.4 above, the Grantor Bank shall not agree to any act or failure to act by any Obligor, or to exercise or refrain from the exercise of any rights or remedies which the Grantor Bank may have under or in respect of any Transaction or any Documentation related thereto without the Purchaser bank's prior consent.

(7) 在进行福费廷交易期间，未经买入行事前书面同意，卖出行不得同意：

During the course of the Forfaiting Transaction, the Grantor Bank should not agree to the following statements without the prior written consent given by the Purchaser Bank:

(a) 债务人对买入行购入债权部分的本金或利息的付款、偿付日期进行延展；

Extend any date (as specified in the relevant Documentation) of any payment of principal or interest in respect of, or reimbursement of, any amounts under any Transaction, or;

(b) 债务人减少买入行购入债权部分的本金的支付或偿付金额。

To reduce the amount of any such payment of principal or such reimbursement.

(8) 基础交易不得涉及联合国、中国政府或者其他政府或国际组织制定的可适用的制裁项目，卖出行不得通过修改或掩饰基础交易背景信息的方式规避反洗钱、制裁合规要求，或其他适用的法律法规、监管规定。如基础交易有合理理由被认为涉及洗钱、恐怖融资或其他违法行为，在当地监管允许的情况下，卖出行有义务向买入行提供其持有或控制的相关信息，以便买入行履行相关的法律义务。

The underlying transaction does not involve any money laundering or terrorist capital or nuclear proliferation or breach any sanctions imposed by the United Nations, the United States government and the People's Republic of China. The Grantor Bank will not modify or cover up any information of the underlying transaction in order to avoid anti-money laundering or sanction check. The Grantor Bank agrees that if the underlying transaction turns out to be involved in money laundering or terrorist capital financing or other illegal activities, it will provide the Purchaser Bank of all information and documents that are within the Grantor bank's possession, custody or control, if permitted by the local regulations, in order for the Purchaser Bank to comply with any applicable laws or regulations.

3.5.3 买入行进一步声明并保证：

The Purchaser Bank further acknowledges and agrees that:

(1) 买入行买入相关债权是完全基于其自身的决定。

Its purchase of the accepted relevant claim depends exclusively on its own credit decisions.

(2) 福费廷交易下买入行对卖出行无追索权。但如果由于下述原因买入行到期未能收到债务人的付款，则卖出行应根据买入行的要求回购债权。

The Forfaiting transaction is made without recourse to the Grantor Bank, unless when there is no payment from the Obligor to the Grantor Bank due to the following reasons.

(a) 卖出行违反了本惯例下的声明、保证、义务或其他条款和条件，或未按照本惯例

履行其职责。

Event A:The Grantor bank＇s breach of representations, warranties, undertakings or any terms and conditions stated in or referred to in The CPF.

(b) 国际信用证项下业务卖出行未能遵守国际商会《跟单信用证统一惯例（UCP600）》或此后更新版本的相关规定。国内信用证业务项下卖出行违反中国人民银行制定的国内信用证有关管理规定。

Event B:The Grantor bank＇s transaction under the import L/C failure to comply with any relevant provisions of the UCP 600 or such later revision as may be adopted by the ICC. The Grantor bank＇s transaction under the domestic L/C failure to comply with any relevant provisions of the rules on Domestic Letter of Credit published by PBOC.

(c) 因法院颁发止付令、禁付令、冻结令或其他具有相同或类似功能的司法命令，无论是最终的或是暂时性的命令，导致买入行未能从债务人处获得偿付。

Event C: A court injunction for fraud or alleged fraud whether such court injunction is a final or an interim injunction that leads to the failure of the Purchaser Bank to get reimbursement from the Obligor.

(d) 因债权本身存在瑕疵导致买入行未能从债务人处获得偿付，例如：卖出行、申请人或受益人欺诈、违约出售给买入行的不是源于正当交易的合法有效债权。

Event D: Defects of titles that harms the creditor＇s rights, such as illegal transaction made by the Grantor Bank/applicant/beneficiary or fraud and other circumstances that leads to the failure of the Purchaser Bank to get reimbursement from the Obligor.

因上述情形，卖出行收到买入行回购通知，卖出行应于收到上述通知后立即将回购款项（包括本金及利息，如有）支付给买入行，并承担买入行可能由此造成的损失。

The consequences of the above events are that, the Purchaser Bank may send repurchase notice to the Grantor Bank, and the Grantor Bank shall pay the Purchaser Bank with repurchase amount (including principal and interest, if any) and bear the losses that the Purchaser Bank may incur without delay.

(3) 买入行保留为完成一笔福费廷交易而向卖出行要求提供其他单据的权利，有关条件应在交易文件中列出。

The Purchaser Bank reserves the right to request for other documentation, which should be listed in the Transaction Document(s), from the Grantor Bank so as to effectuate a proper

discounting.

3.5.4 本惯例第 3.5 条规定的保证和声明在买卖双方每份交易文件中重复适用，在交易文件签署之日生效。

The warranties and representations set out in this Clause 3.5 of the CPF are made on the date hereof and are deemed repeated by each party hereof on the date of each Transaction Document(s).

3.6 通知与送达

Notices and delivery:

3.6.1 书面通信。本惯例项下或与本惯例有关的任何通知、请求、要求或其他通信应以书面形式通过传真、电子邮件或信函形式发出，除非另有声明。

Communications in writing: Any notice, request, demand or other communication to be made under or in connection with the CPF shall be made in writing and, unless otherwise stated, may be made by fax, e-mail or letter.

3.6.2 联系资料选用。与发起人签订的《福费廷服务主合同》及买卖双方交易文件中预留地址可用于递送书面通知。

Contact details. The contact details demonstrated in the *Master Forfaiting Service Contract* signed with the Originator or the Transaction Document(s) between the Trading parties are made for delivery and reception of writing notices.

3.6.3 联系资料变更。交易中任何一方联系人和联系方式如有变动，应在变更发生日之前通过传真或电子邮件通知对方和所有交易对手，否则视为原联系资料仍有效。

Contact detail change. If the contact details of any party in forfaiting transaction are changed, the changed party should notify the other party and all counterparties by fax or e-mail before the change, otherwise the previous contact detail is still effective.

3.6.4 送达。缔约一方发送给另一方本协议项下或与本惯例有关的任何通信或文件仅在下列情况下有效：

Delivery. Any communication or document made or delivered by one Party to the other Party under or in connection with the "CPF" will only be effective:

(1) 通过快递或专人递送的，以签收视为送达。

(a)If sent by post or by hand, it shall be deemed to be delivered upon *signature or seal by the receiver*.

(2) 通过传真送达的，当收到清晰可读文件并同时发出送达确认函时，如果该日期在送达地为非工作日，此类通知、请求或其他通讯均视为在该送达地第二个工作日送达。

(b)If sent by fax, when received in legible form dispatched with a simultaneous confirmation of transmission, provided that if such day is not Business day in the place to delivery, such notice, demand or other communication shall be deemed to be delivered on the next following Business Day at such place.

(3) 通过电子邮件送达的，当电子邮箱记录显示已发送，该通知应视为收到。

(c)If sent by e-mail, e-mail notice shall be deemed received when actually delivered to the recipient as demonstrated by "sent records".

四、准据法、争议解决和主导语言

Article 4.Governing Laws, Disputes Resolution and Ruling Language

本惯例用于 SWIFT 系统的电文由英文书就，用于中国人民银行大小额支付系统的电文由中文书就。其余内容均由中、英双语书就，福费廷交易的准据法、诉讼或仲裁地和主导语言可由买卖双方在交易文件中约定，如中英文版本间存在任何差异，以交易文件约定为准，交易文件没有约定主导语言的，以中文为准。除非交易文件有另行约定，合同的履行地为深圳。交易文件没有约定争议解决方式或准据法的，适用中华人民共和国法律，在深圳诉讼。

The Message for SWIFT is in English. The Message for HVPS is in Chinese, and the other text of the CPF are made in both Chinese and English . The governing laws, litigation or arbitration place and ruling language of forfaiting transaction may be negotiated between Trading parties in the Transaction Documents.

In case of any discrepancy between the English and Chinese version, the ruling language that expressly indicated in Transaction Documents shall prevail, In case that the ruling language had no convention expressly indicated, it's the Chinese version that shall prevail.

In case that the governing laws or disputes resolution had no convention expressly indicated, the forfaiting transaction shall be governed by and construed in accordance with the laws of P.R.China. The disputes shall be resolved through litigation. The parties agree that the place of performance of this Contract and forum of jurisdiction shall be in the City of Shenzhen.

五、信息保密

Article 5.Mutual Non-disclosure

5.1 保密信息

Confidential Information:

"保密信息"包括一方（"披露方"）向另一方（"接收方"）以口头方式、可视方式、电子或书面形式披露的任何和所有保密的技术和商业信息。该等保密信息包括但不限于工商客户资料、单据、信用证。

The term "Confidential Information" shall include and mean any and all confidential technical and business information disclosed by one Party ("Disclosing Party") to the other ("Receiving Party") orally, visually, electronically or in writing. Such Confidential Information may include, but is not limited to, names and information of beneficiary and applicant, documentation, L/C.

5.2 披露限制：

Restrictions of Disclosure:

接收方在未获得披露方的事先书面同意的情况下不得向任何人披露全部或部分保密信息，但下列情形除外：

Receiving Party shall not divulge any such Confidential Information to anyone without the prior written consent of the Disclosing Party, except in the following conditions:

（1）适用法律法规、司法部门或监管机构依法要求披露的；

Events A:Is required to be disclosed by law or by any government agency who has jurisdiction pursuant to an order to produce or in the course of a legal proceeding pursuant to a lawful request for discovery provided;

（2）除非因福费廷业务或外部审计而必须得到专业顾问的服务，而由此专业顾问必须知晓该等保密信息外，不得向上述机构／人员披露保密信息；并且，接受方在向上述机构／人员披露保密信息时，应要求其签订与本惯例条款同样严格的保密协议，以确保保密信息的保密性。

Events B: The Receiving Party shall not disclose the Confidential Information to its Professional Advisers except for them whose services are required for the purpose of Forfaiting transaction or external audit, and such disclosure shall be made only on a need-to-know basis. In addition, the Receiving Party shall execute a confidentiality agreement on terms no less strict than those set out herein prior to disclosing Confidential Information to such institutions/staffs to ensure the confidentiality of Confidential Information.

（3）因询报价需要，向银行披露债务人名称、承兑币种金额、融资期限、标的货物 /服务、行业归属、到期日、起息日、转手次数、意向价格、是否涉及关联交易、融资 (金融) 租赁、发票或提单早于开证日期 3 个月、无运输单据、涉及小微企业、转口、NRA、OSA、两头在外、行政事业收据、买卖双方均为贸易公司、涉及政府融资平台和服务标的为进口代理费，除以上要点外其他信息不得披露。

Events C: Is required for the purpose of request for quotation, disclose name of Obligor, acceptance amount & currency, Tenor, Goods/Services, Industry classification, maturity date, value date, hands, price, affiliated or unaffiliated; this L/C is under the finance lease; invoice or bill of lading before 3 months prior to the date of issue, no transport document, financing for small and micro enterprises, intermediary trade; Non-Resident Account, Offshore Accounting; neither applicant nor beneficiary in the mainland China, administrative receipts in lieu of invoices, both applicant and beneficiary are trading companies; relateing to government financing platform and goods/service of domestic L/C is import agency fee to other bank. No other information should be released except those mentioned above.

5.3 本惯例所涉及的保密义务在本惯例或福费廷业务终止后仍然有效。

The confidentiality obligation involved in the CPF shall be valid after the termination of the CPF or the Forfaiting transaction.

六、本惯例发起人

发起人 (金融信息服务商)：深圳市投友亲金融信息服务有限公司

Originator(Broker)：Universe Trade Finance Information Service Co., Ltd.

有权签字人：史翔　　　　　　职务：总经理

Authorized officer: Shi Xiang　　　Title: General manager

统一社会信用代码 /Company No.：91440300358781745Y

办公地址：福建省福州市鼓楼区桂枝里 5 号 106 室

Office address: Room 106, No.5 Guizhi Road, Gulou District, Fuzhou City, Fujian Province, China

电话 /Tel：+86-18950218792(首选 /Preferred);+86-15280061898(备用 /standby)

+86-17859192809(备用 /standby)

Email：shixiang@forfaiting.ltd

附件 1: 福费廷申请书

Appendix 1: Offer Letter

中文版 /Chinese version:

福费廷申请书

（用于卖出行向买入行发出区块链电文或纸质文件，纸质文件需签字盖章）

（备注：有关选项列于"□"后，需要的请保留在文件中，不用的选项和所有"□"请删除）致：＿＿＿＿＿＿＿＿＿＿＿＿＿银行□＿＿＿＿＿＿＿＿＿＿＿＿＿分行（买入行）

根据我们最近的电话 / 邮件沟通，并遵循深圳市投友亲金融信息服务公司编著的《寰宇贸融福费廷惯例3.9版》[ISBN: 978-7-5615-7173-6]（以下简称"惯例"）的条件和条款，我行拟在你行收到符合要求的单据后以无追索权的方式卖出以下业务：

我行业务文号：（备注：卖出行自行编号）

1. 业务明细

(1) □ 国际信用证 ☑国内信用证 □ 其他：＿＿＿＿＿＿＿＿，编号：＿＿＿＿＿＿＿

(2) 销售合同号：＿＿＿＿＿＿＿＿＿＿＿

(3) 申请人：＿＿＿＿＿＿＿＿＿＿＿

(4) 受益人：＿＿＿＿＿＿＿＿＿＿＿

(5) 货物 / 服务：＿＿＿＿＿＿＿＿＿＿＿

(6) 债务人（承兑行、保兑行等）：＿＿＿＿＿＿＿＿＿＿＿

(7) 承兑金额及币种：＿＿＿＿＿＿＿＿＿＿＿

(8) 期限：＿＿＿＿＿＿＿＿＿＿＿

(9) 备注：＿＿＿＿＿＿＿＿＿＿＿

2. 价格要素

(1) 卖断金额及币种：＿＿＿＿＿＿＿＿＿（大小写均可，如 CNY100000000.00/ 人民币壹亿元整）

(2) 贴现率：直接贴现法□ ____% p.a.(包含风险承担费____% p.a.) □ Libor+ ____ BP
(包含风险承担费 ____ BP)

(3) 结息方式：□预扣□利随本清□其他：

(4) 起息日：_____

(5) 到期日：_____

(6) 宽限期：____天

(7) 汇款费：_____(备注：如没有填0.00下同)

(8) 电报费：_____

(9) 承诺费：_____

(10)(币种 & 金额)_____的预扣费将从贴现款中扣除，以支付任何可能的银行收费。如果银行手续费超过所述金额，在我行要求的情况下，你行必须立即支付不足金额。

(11) 预提所得税：_____

(12) 金融信息服务费由□我行 □你行承担，金额：_____

(13) 款项净额：_____

3. 单据

☑经证实的编号为（填信用证编号）的信用证及全部修改电文，其中国际信用证遵循UCP最新版本，国内信用证遵循中国人民银行最新版管理规定（通过传真、电子邮件或区块链信用证系统）要求：☑签字；☑盖章；□原件；☑加盖 Certified True Copy 或与原件相符章之复印件；

☑经证实的商业发票和运输单据；（通过传真、电子邮件或区块链信用证系统）要求：☑签字；☑盖章；□原件；☑加盖 Certified True Copy 或与原件相符章之复印件；

☑经证实的债务人承兑确认文件（通过传真、电子邮件或区块链信用证系统）要求：☑签字；☑盖章；□原件；☑加盖 Certified True Copy 或与原件相符章之复印件；

☑以你行为受益人的债权转让书；（通过加押 SWIFT、区块链电文或人行大额支付系统确认电文）

☑经证实的以你行为受益人，我行发给债务人的债权转让通知书。（通过传真、电子邮件或区块链信用证系统）要求：☑签字；☑盖章；□原件；☑加盖 Certified True Copy 或与原件相符章之复印件；

□卖出行出具的贸易背景真实性□和是否关联交易说明（通过传真、电子邮件或区块链系统）要求：☑签字；□盖章；☑原件；□加盖 Certified True Copy 或与原件相符章之复印件；

（备注：如有其他要求请自行补充）

4.卖出行联系资料：

联系人：

电话：

传真：

电邮：

通讯地址：

5.适用法律

此交易受;☑中华人民共和国;□英国;□其他:(双方自行商定后填写，例如中国香港、新加坡、美国纽约等)法律约束并据此进行解释。(注意：非跨境交易必须适用本地区法律)

6.争议解决

□中国国际经济贸易仲裁委员会仲裁

凡因本次福费廷交易引起的或与本次福费廷交易有关的任何争议，均应提交☑中国国际经济贸易仲裁委员会□中国国际经济贸易仲裁委员会香港仲裁中心，按照申请仲裁时该会现行有效的仲裁规则以中文进行仲裁。仲裁裁决是终局的，对双方均有约束力。

□香港国际仲裁中心仲裁

凡因本次福费廷交易所引起的或与之相关的任何争议、纠纷、分歧或索赔，包括交易、合同及惯例的存在、效力、解释、履行、违反或终止，或因本次福费廷交易引起的或与之相关的任何非合同性争议，均应提交由香港国际仲裁中心管理的仲裁，并按照提交仲裁通知时有效的《香港国际仲裁中心机构仲裁规则》最终解决。本仲裁条款适用的法律为香港法，仲裁地应为香港，仲裁员人数为□一名☑三名。仲裁程序应按照☑中文□英文来进行。仲裁裁决是终局的，对双方均有约束力。

□新加坡国际仲裁中心仲裁

凡因本次福费廷交易而产生的或与之有关的任何争议，包括交易、合同及惯例的存在、效力或终止等任何问题，应提交新加坡国际仲裁中心，并按其现行有效的规则，在新加坡进行最终仲裁。本合同签订后，若新加坡国际仲裁中心对其仲裁规则有所修订，则按新加坡国际仲裁中心已通过且生效的最新修订规则进行仲裁。新加坡国际仲裁中心的现行规则或上述修订规则应被视为本条的一部分。本仲裁条款适用的法律为新加坡法，仲裁员人数为□一名☑三名。仲裁程序应按照☑中文□英文来进行。仲裁裁决是终局的，

对双方均有约束力。

☑诉讼：争议应通过法院诉讼解决，任何一方有权在□买入行所在地□卖出行所在地☑被告所在地□其他 :(双方自行商定后填写 , 例如北京、香港、新加坡等) 法院提起诉讼。

7. 主导语言

在交易涉及的惯例和有关交易文件中，如中英文表述存在差异，以☑中文□英文为准。

8. 合同签订地与履行地

买卖双方同意该笔福费廷业务合同签订地为□买入行所在地□卖出行所在地□其他 :(双方自行商定后填写 , 例如北京、香港、新加坡等)，合同履行地为□买入行所在地□卖出行所在地□其他: (双方自行商定后填写 , 例如北京、香港、新加坡等)。

9. 截止日期

如你行经办机构在_____年____月____日之前收到符合要求的单据，你行应在 (填数字 , 如壹) 个工作日之内根据我行指示向我行支付该笔业务的净额。请在 (填数字 , 如壹) 个工作日内向我行确认上述申请，否则该申请将失效。

祝：商祺

卖出行 :(盖章)

有权签字人:

年 月 日

英文版 /English version:

Offer Letter

(To be prepared on the Grantor bank's via authenticated SWIFT or block chain message)

(Note: please check all the options which are listed after ""□"" you need to save and delete the other unnecessary options after ""□"")

Date：_____

To：_____(the Purchaser Bank)

20：Our Reference Number:_____

21：

79：Referring to our recent correspondence/telephone discussion, and subject to the terms and conditions of the Universe Trade Finance Customs and Practice for Forfaiting version

3.9(ISBN:978-7-5615-7173-6, hereinafter called the CPF) that Compiled by Universe Trade Finance Information Service Co., Ltd., we hereby offer to sell the following transaction subject to receipt of satisfactory Documentation to you on without recourse basis.

1. Transaction particulars

(a) ☐ Import L/C ☑ Domestic L/C ☐ Other:_____ under No. _____

(b) Sales contract No. _____

(c) Applicant: _____

(d) Beneficiary: _____

(e) Goods/Services: _____

(f) Obligor Bank(s) (e.g. Accepting Bank/Confirming Bank, etc)：_____

(g) Acceptance Amount & Currency: _____

(h) Tenor/ Maturity: _____

(i) Remark: _____

2. Pricing elements

(a) Forfaiting Currency & Amount: _____

(b) Discounting Rate: straight discount

☐_____% p.a.(including risk undertaking fee____% p.a.)

☐_____ plus_____ BP (including risk undertaking fee _____ BP)

(c) Interest Settlement: ☐ Value date ☐ Maturity date ☐ Other：

(d) Value date: _____

(e) Maturity date: _____

(f) Grace days: _____

(g) Remittance Fee: _____

(h) Cable Fee: _____

(i) Commitment Fee(if any): _____

(j) A Pre-deduction of _____will be deducted from the discount proceeds to cover any possible banking charges. If the banking charges exceed the said amount, we will reimburse youthe shortfall immediately upon our request.

(k) Withholding Tax accruing: _____

(l) Broker Services Fee shall be borne by ☐ us ☐ you,Amount: _____(if any)

(m) Net Proceeds: _____

3. Documentation

☑Certified true copy of L/C , No. _____ and amendments (Domestic L/C should be subject to the rules on Domestic Letter of Credit latest version published by PBOC,Import L/C should be subject to UCP latest version published by ICC) ; (via fax/block chain based Letter of Credit system/Email)documents required: ☑ Signature; ☑ Seal; ☐ Original; ☑ Certified True Copy

☑ Certified true copy of commercial invoices and/or transport documents; (via fax/block chain based Letter of Credit system/Email)documents required: ☑ Signature; ☑ Seal ☐ Original; ☑ Certified True Copy

☑ Certified true copy of Obligor bank's confirmation of acceptance; (via fax/block chain based Letter of Credit system/Email)documents required: ☑ Signature; ☑ Seal; ☐ Original; ☑ Certified True Copy

☑Letter of Assignment in favor of you; (via Authenticated SWIFT/block chain based Letter of Credit system)

☑ Certified true copy of Notice of Assignment in favor of you from us to the Obligor Bank. (via fax/Email)documents required: ☑ Signature; ☑ Seal; ☐ Original; ☑ Certified True Copy

☐ Certificate of trade authenticity ☑ and ☑ affiliated/unaffiliated transactions issued by us (via fax/block chain based Letter of Credit system/Email)documents required:

☑ Signature; ☑ Seal; ☑ Original; ☐ Certified True Copy

(Note:If you have any other demand, please add it yourself)

4. Our contact details

Contact Person:

Tel:

Fax:

Email:

Postal Address:

5. Governing Law

This Transaction shall be governed by and construed in accordance with the laws of ☑ P.R.China ☐ England ☐ Other:(the law agreed by trading parties,e.g. Singapore, State of New

27

York, U.S.A.etc.).(Notice: Non cross border transactions must governed by local law)

6.Disputes

☐ Arbitration under the CIETAC's arbitration rules:

Any dispute arising from or in connection with this transaction shall be submitted to ☑ China International Economic and Trade Arbitration Commission (CIETAC) ☐ CIETAC Hong Kong Arbitration Centre for arbitration which shall be conducted in accordance with the CIETAC's arbitration rules in effect at the time of applying for arbitration in Chinese language. The arbitral award is final and binding upon both parties.

☐ Arbitration under the HKIAC Administered Arbitration Rules:

Any dispute, controversy, difference or claim arising out of or relating to this transaction,contract and the CPF, including the existence, validity, interpretation, performance, breach or termination thereof or any dispute regarding non-contractual obligations arising out of or relating to it shall be referred to and finally resolved by arbitration administered by the Hong Kong International Arbitration Centre (HKIAC) under the HKIAC Administered Arbitration Rules in force when the Notice of Arbitration is submitted. The law of this arbitration clause shall be Hong Kong law. The seat of arbitration shall be Hong Kong. The number of arbitrators shall be ☐ one ☑ three. The arbitration proceedings shall be conducted in ☑ Chinese ☐ English The arbitral award is final and binding upon both parties.

☐ Arbitration under the SIAC Rules:

Any dispute arising out of or in connection with this transaction, contract and the CPF, including any question regarding its existence, validity or termination, shall be referred to and finally resolved by arbitration administered by the Singapore International Arbitration Centre ("SIAC") in accordance with the Arbitration Rules of the Singapore International Arbitration Centre ("SIAC Rules") for the time being in force, which rules are deemed to be incorporated by reference in this clause. The law of this arbitration clause shall be Singapore law.The number of arbitrators shall be ☐ one ☑ three. The arbitration proceedings shall be conducted in ☐ Chinese ☑ English. The arbitral award is final and binding upon both parties.

☑ Litigation: The disputes shall be resolved through litigation. Any party can bring such dispute to the court at the place where ☐ the Purchaser Bank is registered ☐ The Grantor Bank is registered ☑ defendant is registered ☐ Other:(the city agreed by trading parties.

e.g.Beijing,Shanghai,Singapore).(Notice:Non-cross-border transactions must litigae in local legal jurisdiction).

7.Ruling language:

In the CPF and transaction documents related to this transaction, in case of any discrepancy between the English and Chinese version, the ☑ Chinese ☐ English version shall prevail;

8.Places of this contract's conclusion and performance

Both parties agree that the place of the Forfaiting transaction contract's conclusion is where ☑ the Purchaser Bank is registered ☐ the Grantor Bank is registered ☑ Other:(the city agreed by trading parties. e.g. Beijing, Shanghai, Singapore).and the place of its performance is ☑ the Purchaser Bank is registered ☐ the Grantor Bank is registered ☑ Other:(the city agreed by trading parties. e.g. Beijing, Shanghai, Singapore).

9. Deadline:

Subject to receipt of satisfactory Documentation at your offices on or before _____, you shall pay us the net proceeds within (one) business day(s) from the date of such receipt according to our instructions.

Please kindly confirm your acceptance of the above offer to us within (one) business day(s) from the date of such receipt, otherwise the offer shall expire.

Best Regards.

_____ (Authorized signature)

For and on behalf of _____

(The Grantor Bank)

附件2: 福费廷确认函

Appendix 2: Forfaiting Confirmation

中文版 /Chinese version:

福费廷确认函

（用于买入行向卖出行回复的区块链电文或纸质文件，纸质文件需签字盖章后生效）

（备注：有关选项列于"□"后，需要的请保留在文件中，不用的选项和所有"□"请删除）

致 _____ 银行□ _____ 分行 (卖出行)

你行文号_____ 的申请书已收悉，现函复如下：

本福费廷确认函遵循深圳市投友亲金融信息服务公司编著的《寰宇贸融福费廷惯例3.9版》[ISBN:978-7-5615-7173-6]。我行现确认接受你行于___年___月___日发来的编号为 (填申请书文号) 的《福费廷申请书》(以下简称"申请书"）。我们将根据该申请书中的条件和条款进行福费廷交易。烦请你行通知债务人：上述款项合计 (填承兑币种和金额)，应按照债务人已承兑的全额款项不扣除任何费用，在到期日当日直接汇至我行账号_____户名_____收款行_____，(□ SWIFT/CIPS:_____ □中国人民银行大额支付系统:_____)。

与上述交易有关的细节和单据以你行提供申请书为准。买入行联系资料：

联系人：

电话：

传真：

电邮：

通讯地址：

祝：商祺

买入行:（盖章）

有权签字人：

年 月 日

英文版 /English version:

Forfaiting Confirmation

(To be prepared on the Purchaser bank's via authenticated SWIFT or block chain message)

(Note: please check all the options which are listed after "□" you need to save and delete the other unnecessary options after "□")

Date：_____

To：_____ (The Grantor Bank)

Attn:_____

20：

21：Our Reference Number: _____

79：Re: Forfaiting Transaction under _____ (Name of Documents) No.

This forfaiting confirmation is subject to Universe Trade Finance Customs and Practice for Forfaiting version 3.9(ISBN:978-7-5615-7173-6,hereinafter called the CPF)that Compiled by Universe Trade Finance Information Service Co., Ltd. We hereby confirm that we accept your Offer Letter that Ref No. Is and Dated (the "Offer"). We will proceed with the Forfaiting transaction according to the terms and conditions in the Offer.

Please send notice to Obligor,The payment for (Currency&Amount) on maturity date shall be effected directly to our bank's account _____ (a/c No._____) with (the name of the bank) (□ SWIFT/CIPS:_____ ☑ CNAPS:_____), for the full face value Obligor have accepted without any deductions whatsoever.

Particulars and documentation in relation to the above-mentioned transaction shall be subject to your Offer.

Our contact details:

Contact Person:

Tel:

Fax:

Email:

Postal Address:

Best Regards.

Yours faithfully,

_____ (Authorized signature)

For and on behalf of _____

(The Purchaser Bank)

附件3: 债权转让书

Appendix 3: Letter of Assignment

英文版 /English version:

Date: _____

To: _____ (The Purchaser Bank)

Letter of Assignment

(Authenticated SWIFT or block chain message)

(Note: please check all the options which are listed after "□" you need to save and delete the other unnecessary options after "□")

Re: _____ (Our Ref. No.)

Re:Assignment of_____ (Currency and Amount) under the L/C No._____honored and accepted/confirmed by_____ Bank(Name of Obligor Bank)

We subject to the Universe Trade Finance Customs and Practice for Forfaiting version 3.9(ISBN: 978-7-5615-7173-6,hereinafter called the CPF) that Compiled by Universe Trade Finance Information Service Co., Ltd. and your Forfaiting Confirmation (dated_____Ref. No._____) in respect of your purchase of the debt/bills under the above mentioned transaction. This is an Assignment.

In consideration of your purchase without recourse, we hereby:

☑ confirm that (Beneficiary's name) has unconditionally and irrevocably transferred its rights and benefits accruing under the transaction to us. Accordingly we hereby unconditionally and irrevocably assign to you all of our right, title and interests under the transaction as well as all of accompanying amendment(s). We hereby represent and warrant to you that we are the sole legal and beneficial owner of the rights hereby transferred.(in case that the Grantor Bank is the counterparty of the Purchaser Bank, save/check the option)

☐ on behalf of (Beneficiary's name), irrevocably and unconditionally transfer to you with full title, guarantee, rights, claims, interest and benefit accruing to us with respect to the accepted amount under the above mentioned transaction, we hereby confirm that we have obtained the unconditional and irrevocable authorization on the above transfer from (Beneficiary's name).

We confirm that the transferred rights are free and clear of any pledge, security interest, claim, set-off, counterclaim, charge or any other encumbrance. This assignment shall by no means transfer our obligation and duty under the transaction to you.(in case that the Beneficiary is the counterparty of the Purchaser Bank, save/check the option)

We hereby represent and warrant that:

☑ We will notify (name of the Obligor Bank) of the transaction to directly pay to you the accepted amount under the transaction or accept your instructions in that regard. Notwithstanding the foregoing, we further confirm that in case of receiving any proceeds under the transaction from the Obligor Bank at maturity, we shall directly pay to you without delay.or your assignees in accordance with your instructions, for the full face value we received and any interests accrued thereon, free of any deduction whatsoever from our side.(In case that the Grantor Bank isn't Obligor,save/check the option)

☐ as the Issuing Bank/Accepting Bank/Confirming Bank of the transaction, we hereby confirm the payment for (currency and amount) on maturity date (yyyy-MM-dd) shall be effected directly to you in accordance with the payment instruction stated in your Forfaiting Confirmation (Dated_____ Ref. No._____)for the full face value, free of any deduction whatsoever from our side.(In case that the Grantor Bank is Obligor,save/check the option)

This Letter of Assignment constitutes an integral part to the above mentioned CPF.

Please pay the Net Proceeds to our bank's account _____(a/c No. _____) with (the name of the bank) (☐ SWIFT/CIPS:_____ ☑ CNAPS:_____),quoting our Ref. No._____.

☐ Please pay the Broker Service fee to broker's account Universe Trade Finance Information Service Co., Ltd.(a/c No. _____) with (the name of the bank) (☐ SWIFT/CIPS: _____ ☑CNAPS:_____) , quoting our Ref. no._____.(In case when Broker Service fee are involved,save/check the option)

☐ We confirm that our bank's chop/seal(s) and/or signature(s) on the offer letter and docs

faxed/scanned to you are authentic and legally binding on us.(In case that there are no reserved seal and signature sample between trading parties,save/check the option)

Best Regards.

Yours faithfully,

_____ (Authorized Signature)

On behalf of _____

(The Grantor Bank)

中文版 /Chinese version:

债权转让书

（用于卖出行向买入行发送的区块链电文或纸质文件，纸质文件需签字盖章后生效）

（备注：有关选项列于"□"后，需要的请保留在文件中，不用的选项和所有"□"请删除）致：_____银行□_____分行（买入行）：

我行文号：_____。

我行遵循深圳市投友亲金融信息服务公司编著的《寰宇贸融福费廷惯例3.9版》[ISBN:978-7-5615-7173-6]（以下简称"惯例"）和你行于____年____月____日发来的编号为（填确认函编号）的《福费廷确认函》向你行转让上述交易在（填信用证编号）号信用证项下经承兑/保兑的债权。

鉴于你行无追索权地受让我行业务：

☑我行确认（受益人）不可撤销地将其在申请业务项下的一切权利和收益转让我行，我行特此向你行无条件地、不可撤销地将我行拥有的在业务及全部修改电文项下的一切权利、所有权、收益转让给你行。我行向你行保证我行是该项权利的唯一合法受益人。（卖出行先对企业放款后卖出的选此项）

□谨代表（受益人）无条件地、不可撤销地转让上述业务项下承兑的一切所有权、担保、权利、索赔、利息和收益，我行特此确认已就上述转让事宜取得（受益人）无条件的、不可撤销的授权。

我行确认该权利可自由转让，不涉及任何质押、担保、索赔、抵消、反诉、费用或任何其他负担。本次转让不得将我行在此业务项下的责任和义务转让给你行。（卖出行不做企业交易对手只做企业代理人的选此项）

我行特此声明并保证：

☑我行将通知债务人 (或填行名) 在付款到期日直接将业务项下承兑金额支付你行，或根据你行指示支付。此外，我行确认：一旦我行在付款到期日收到债务人的针对该业务下的款项，我行将立即将所收到的款项全额直接支付你行或根据你行指示支付，我行将不扣除任何费用。(卖出行不是债务人的选此项)

□我行是该笔业务的开证行 / 承兑行 / 保兑行，我行确认在付款到期日 (填日期，格式 :yyyy-MM-dd) 将根据你行于 (填日期，格式 yyyy-MM-dd) 发给我行编号为 (填确认函文号) 的《福费廷确认函》所述还款指示直接支付承兑款项全额到你行，我行将不扣除任何费用。(卖出行就是债务人的选此项)

本债权转让书是上述惯例不可分割的组成部分。其他未尽事宜按照惯例解释和办理。

请将款项净额支付到我行账号_____户名____收款行_____，(□ SWIFT/CIPS:_____ □中国人民银行大额支付系统：_____) 并引用我行编号：_____

□请将金融信息服务费支付到金融信息服务商账号_____户名：深圳市投友亲金融信息服务有限公司,收款行_____，开户行：(□ SWIFT/CIPS:_____ □中国人民银行大额支付系统：_____) 并引用我行编号：_____(如有金融信息服务费选此项)。

□我行确认在传真或扫描给你行的《福费廷申请书》和单据上的我方印章和 / 或签字是真实的，具有法律约束力。(如买卖双方无预留印鉴选此项)

祝商祺

有权签字人：

卖出行:（盖章）

年 月 日

附件4: 转让通知书

Appendix 4: Notice of Assignment

英文版 /English version:

(Note: please check all the options which are listed after "□" you need to save and delete the other unnecessary options after "□")

Notice of Assignment

(Authenticated SWIFT or block chain message)

Date: _____

To : _____ (name of the Obligor Bank)

Re: The L/C under No. _____ for (Currency and Amount) duly honored and accepted/confirmed by you mature on (yyyy-MM-dd).

Please be advised that the rights and proceeds of the L/C have been irrevocably and unconditionally assigned to (the Purchaser Bank name) (hereinafter referred to as the "Assignee"). On Maturity Date, please effect the payment directly to Assignee's account No. _____ with _____ bank (□ SWIFT/CIPS: _____ √ CNAPS: _____), quoting their ref. No. _____ .

Therefore please confirm by return authenticated SWIFT directly to Assignee(SWIFT: _____):

Your kind acknowledgment on above assignment,and

The payment on maturity date shall be effected directly to Assignee in accordance with above payment instruction for the full face value, without any deductions.

Notwithstanding the foregoing, the captioned assignment has taken into effect upon the mutual agreement/contract between Assignee and us and shall not be prejudiced by any action or

inaction of you.

Best regards.

_____ (Authorized Signature)

On behalf of _____

(The Grantor Bank)

翻译稿仅供参考/translation version for reference only:

转让通知书

（翻译稿，仅供参考）

致_____银行 (债务人)：

关于信用证编号：_____，由你行承兑 / 保兑的将于 年 月 日到期的信用证项下**币种 & 金额**的款项

请注意，单据的权利和收益已被不可撤销地无条件转让给 (买入行)，以下简称 "受让人"。

请在到期日将款项付至受让人的账号为：_____ 收款行_____，(□ SWIFT/CIPS:_____ ☑中国人民银行大额支付系统：_____) 引用受让人业务编号_____。

因此，请通过加押 SWIFT 直接向受让人 (SWIFT:_____) 回复确认电如下：

你行确认已知悉上述转让。

你行将根据上述付款指示在到期日，直接向受让人支付款项，不作任何扣减。

除了上述情况外，(买入行) 和我行之间签订的转让协议已经生效，其效力不受你行行为影响。

诚致问候。

有权签字人：

卖出行：

中文版 /Chinese version:

转让通知书

（用于卖出行向买入行发送的区块链电文或纸质文件，纸质文件需签字盖章后生效）

（备注：有关选项列于"□"后，需要的请保留在文件中，不用的选项和所有"□"请删除）

编号：

_____银行股份有限公司□_____分行（债务人）：

我行是你行承兑的编号为_____的□国内□国际信用证项下债权的持有行，我行已将该信用证项下一切权利及款项不可撤销地转让给_____银行□_____分行（以下简称"买入行"），特此通知你行，并请你行在承兑到期日将承兑款项划转至买入行账户。

信用证编号：

承兑金额：

申请人全称：

受益人全称：

承兑付款日期：

如你行对上述信息确认无误，请你行选择通过 SWIFT 加押电文、区块链信用证系统自由格式电文或中国人民银行大额支付系统自由格式电文发送如下中文或英文回执信息至买入行，并在承兑到期日按时将承兑金额划转至如下账户：

户名：

开户行：

账号：

支付系统行号:(□ SWIFT/CIPS:_____ □中国人民银行大额支付系统：_____)

SWIFT 或区块链信用证系统回执英文信息：We have taken notice of and agreed with our irrevocable and unconditional assignment of all rights, title and interest in respect of the L/C under No._____ for (Currency and Amount) to you.

The payment on maturity date shall be effected directly to you, A/C No. _____ with _____ (□ SWIFT/CIPS: _____ ☑ CNAPS: _____) quoting Ref. No. _____ or in accordance with the payment instruction that we will receive from you, for the full face value, without any deductions whatsoever.

中国人民银行大额支付系统或区块链信用系统回执中文信息：我行已获悉我行承兑的编号为＿＿＿＿＿＿＿＿＿＿＿的信用证项下承兑款项债权由 (填卖出行) 银行□＿＿＿＿＿分行转让至你行并对编号为：＿＿＿＿＿＿＿＿＿＿的转让通知书内容无异议，我行将在承兑到期日将承兑款项 (填承兑金额 , 如 CNY100000000.00) 划转至你行指定账户＿＿＿＿＿＿＿＿＿＿＿＿＿＿ (账号)。

买入行联系资料：

联系人：

电话：

传真：

电邮：

通讯地址：

特此通知

卖出行：＿＿＿＿＿银行□＿＿＿＿＿分行 (盖章)

年 月 日

深圳市投友亲金融信息服务有限公司
Universe Trade Finance Information Service Co., Ltd.
网站 /Website:www.forfaiting.ltd; www.forfaiting.shop

附件5: 中国人民银行大额支付系统福费廷申请书确认电文稿
Appendix 5:Confirmation of Offer Letter via HVPS：

中文版 /Chinese version:

（备注：有关选项列于"□"后，需要的请保留在电文中，不用的选项和所有"□"请删除）

我行根据《寰宇贸融福费廷惯例3.9版》[ISBN:978-7-5615-7173-6] 和 (填编号) 号的福费廷申请书约定拟将 (填债务人，名字太长的可考虑缩写但不要有歧义如某商合肥、某州农商) 承兑的☑国内□国际证编号: (填信用证号) 项下于 (填到期日含宽限期, 格式 :yyyy-MM-dd) 还款的债权 (填到期还款金额，如 CNY100000000.00) 卖断你行☑诉讼□仲裁地 (根据福费廷申请书勾选和填写，无用的选项可删除，例如某州)。

我行保证申请书上签章真实，请 (根据申请书填写，如遇节假日要加上，如填1) 日内复。

英文翻译稿仅供参考 /English translation version for reference only:

According to the terms and conditions of the Universe Trade Finance Customs and Practice for Forfaiting version 3.9(ISBN:978-7-5615-7173-6) Compiled by Universe Trade Finance Information Service Co., Ltd. and Offer Letter whose Ref .No. is _____ , we offer to sell on a without recourse basis ☑ Import L/C □ Domestic L/C under No. _____ accepted by (Obligor) Bank, Maturity date is yyyy-MM-dd,amount:(Currency&Amount), □ Arbitration ☑ Litigation place: _____ We confirm that our bank's chop/seal(s) and/or signature(s) on the offer letter and docs faxed/scanned to you are authentic. Please kindly confirm your acceptance of the above offer to us within _____ business day(s) from the date of such receipt.

附件6: 中国人民银行大额支付系统福费廷确认函确认电文稿

Appendix 6:Confirmation of Forfaiting Confirmation via HVPS：

中文版 /Chinese version:

（备注：有关选项列于"□"后，需要的请保留在电文中，不用的选项和所有"□"请删除）

你行 (填申请书编号) 号《福费廷申请书》收悉，融资 (填实际融资天数含宽限期) 天 , 货描 : (如 : 燃油), 价格 (填综合报价)，费用共 (填总费用含金融信息服务费 , 如 CNY900.00) □预收□后收息 , 按《寰宇贸融福费廷惯例3.9版》[ISBN:978-7-5615-7173-6] 办理 , 我行 (填确认函编号) 号《福费廷确认函》已接受你行上述申请并寄回你行 , 我行保证确认函上签章真实。

英文翻译稿仅供参考 /English translation version for reference only:

We hereby confirm thatwe accept your Offer Letter that Ref.No. is _____ Tenor:(days) ☑ Goods □ Services:(e.g.:fuel oil),Pricing: _____ %,total fees:CNY _____ ,Interest Settlement:RValue date □ Maturity date,(you must issue the Certificate of trade authenticity and unaffiliated transactions). We will proceed with the Forfaiting transaction according to the terms and conditions in the Offer and Universe Trade Finance Customs and Practice for Forfaiting version 3.9(ISBN:978-7-5615-7173-6), The Forfaiting Confirmation that Ref.No. is _____ has been replied. We confirm that our bank's chop/seal(s) and/or signature(s) on the Forfaiting Confirmation to you are authentic.

附件7: 中国人民银行大额支付系统债权转让确认电文稿

Appendix 7:Confirmation of Letter of Assignment via HVPS：

中文版 /Chinese version:

（备注：有关选项列于"□"后，需要的请保留在电文中，不用的选项和所有"□"请删除）

我行根据《寰宇贸融福费廷惯例3.9版》[ISBN:978-7-5615-7173-6] 和 (填编号) 号债权转让书约定将 (填债务人, 名字太长的可考虑缩写但不要有歧义如某商合肥) 承兑的 (填信用证号) 号□国内□国际证项下一切权益转让你行。已通知债务人于 (填到期日不含宽限期, 格式: yyyy-MM-dd) 向你行还款 (填到期还款金额, 如 CNY100000000.00)。我行保证有关签章真实, 请付贴现款 (填申请书的款项净额, 如 CNY99649000.00)。

英文翻译稿仅供参考 /English translation version for reference only:

According to the terms and conditions of the Universe Trade Finance Customs and Practice for Forfaiting version 3.9(ISBN:978-7-5615-7173-6) compiled by Universe Trade Finance Information Service Co., Ltd. and Letter of Assignment whose Ref.No. is _____ , we shall sell on a without recourse basis □ Import L/C ☑ Domestic L/C under No. _____ accepted by _____ bank. We had sent notice to Obligor,the payment for (amount) on maturity date (yyyy-MM-dd) shall be effected directly to you. We confirm that our bank's chop/seal(s) and/or signature(s) on the Letter of Assignment and docs faxed/scanned to you are authentic and have sent to you. Please pay the Net Proceeds _____ to our account.

附件8：中国人民银行大额支付系统转让通知电文

Appendix 8:Confirmation of Notice of Assignment via HVPS

中文版 /Chinese version:

（备注：有关选项列于"□"后，需要的请保留在电文中，不用的选项和所有"□"请删除）

你行承兑的 (填信用证号) 号☑国内□国际证项下承兑款项债权已由我行无条件不可撤销地转让至 (填买入行) 银行□＿＿＿＿＿分行，请在到期日将承兑款项划转至账号 :(按还款路径填写) □ SWIFT:＿＿＿＿＿＿☑CNAPS:＿＿＿＿＿＿＿。烦请向受让行确认。我行保证 (填编号) 号转让通知书上签章真实且已寄往你行。

英文翻译稿仅供参考 /English translation version for reference only:

The rights and proceeds of The ☑ Import L/C □ Domestic L/C under No. ＿＿＿＿＿ for (amount) honored and accepted/confirmed by you has been irrevocably and unconditionally assigned to (the Purchaser Bank name).On Maturity Date, please effect the payment directly to Assignee's account No. ＿＿＿＿＿ (□ SWIFT:＿＿＿＿＿ ☑CNAPS:＿＿＿＿＿), and please confirm by return message via SWIFT/HVPS directly to Purchaser Bank. We confirm that our bank's chop/seal(s) and/or signature(s) on the Notice of Assignment whose Ref.No. is ＿＿＿＿＿ to you are authentic and had send to you.

附件9: 预留印鉴及签字样本

Appendix 9: Reserved seal and signature sample

中文版 /Chinese version:

（备注：有关选项列于"□"后，需要的请保留在文件中，不用的选项和所有"□"请删除）

预留印鉴及签字样本

甲方：＿＿＿＿＿＿银行股份有限公司□＿＿＿＿＿＿分行

乙方：＿＿＿＿＿＿银行股份有限公司□＿＿＿＿＿＿分行

甲乙双方同意凡根据深圳市投友亲金融信息服务公司编著的《寰宇贸融福费廷惯例3.9版》[ISBN:978-7-5615-7173-6] 办理福费廷业务时预留业务印鉴及签字样本如下：

甲方业务联系方式	甲方有权签字人签字样本：
部门：	
联系人：	
电话：	（甲方用章样本）
传真：	
Email：	
乙方业务联系方式	乙方有权签字人签字样本：
部门：	
联系人：	
电话：	（乙方用章样本）
传真：	
Email：	

本预留印鉴及签字样本一式两份，甲乙双方各执一份，扫描件与原件具有同等效力。

甲方单位公章：　　　　　　　　　　乙方单位公章：

授权人签字：　　　　　　　　　　　授权人签字：

日期：　　　　　　　　　　　　　　日期：

![Universe Trade Finance logo] 深圳市投友亲金融信息服务有限公司
Universe Trade Finance Information Service Co., Ltd.
网站 /Website:www.forfaiting.ltd; www.forfaiting.shop

英文版 /English version:

(Note: please check all the options which are listed after "□" you need to save and delete the other unnecessary options after "□")

Reserved seal and signature sample message)

Party A: _____ Bank □_____ branch

Party B: _____ Bank □_____ branch

Both parties agree to use the following seal(if any) and signature sample for Forfaiting transaction subject to the Universe Trade Finance Customs and Practice for Forfaiting version 3.9(ISBN:978-7-5615-7173-6) that Compiled by Universe Trade Finance Information Service Co., Ltd. :

Party A's contact details:	Authorized signatures of party A：
Department：	
Contacts:	
Tel:	(seal of party A)(if any)
Fax:	
Email:	
Party B's contact details:	Authorized signature of party B：
Department：	
Contacts:	
Tel:	(seal of party B)(if any)
Fax:	
Email:	

This documentation for Reserved seal and signature samples is in two copies, Party A and Party B have one of each. Scanned copies hold the same legal effect as the originals.

Authorized Signature and Seal(if any)：   Authorized Signature and Seal(if any)：

For and on behalf of Party A   For and on behalf of Party B

Signed this day of   Signed this day of

服务合同范本（供签约行和发起人签署）/Service Contract Model(Signed by Licensed Bank and Originator):

合同编号 /**Contract No.**_____

福费廷服务主合同
Master Forfaiting Service Contract

甲方（签约行）： _____**银行（在**_____**国注册并存续的银行）**

Party A (The "Licensed Bank"): _____ **bank, a bank duly registered and existing under the laws of** _____

有权签字人： _____ **职务：** _____

Authorized officer: _____ **Title:** _____

统一社会信用代码 / 公司注册编号 / Company No. _____

通讯地址： _____

Postal Address: _____

电话 /Tel： + _____ - _____

传真 /Fax： + _____ - _____

Email： _____

乙方（发起人和金融信息服务商）：深圳市投友亲金融信息服务有限公司（在中华人民共和国注册并存续的公司）

Party B (The "Originator" and "Broker"):Universe Trade Finance Information Service Co., Ltd., a company duly registered and existing under the laws of P.R.China

有权签字人：史翔   **职务：总经理**

Authorized officer: Shi Xiang   **Title: General manager**

统一社会信用代码 /Company No：91440300358781745Y

通讯地址：福建省福州市鼓楼区桂枝里5号106室

Postal Address: Room 106, No.5 Guizhi Road,Gulou District, Fuzhou City, Fujian Province, China

电话 /Tel：+86-18950218792(**首选** /Preferred);+86-15280061898(**备用** /standby)

+86-17859192809(**备用** /standby)

Email：**shixiang@forfaiting.ltd**

为促进福费廷业务良性发展，甲乙双方在平等互利的基础上，签订《福费廷服务主合同》(以下简称"本合同")。鉴于：

1. 乙方作为《寰宇贸融福费廷惯例3.9 版》(以下简称"惯例"，详见附件1) 的作者和发起人，同意授权甲方使用并遵循惯例办理福费廷业务。

2. 乙方是福费廷业务的信息中介。

3. 甲方作为惯例签约行有意取得惯例使用权用于与同为签约行的交易对手开展遵循惯例的福费廷业务。

因此，甲乙双方就本合同订立如下条款，以资共同遵守：

This Master Forfaiting Service Contract (the "Contract")is entered into and made effective by and between Party A and Party B, based on equality and mutual benefit to common benign development of forfaiting business. WITNESSED:

Whereas, Party B is the author and originator of Universe Trade Finance Customs and Practice for Forfaiting version 3.9 (the "CPF", specified in Appendix 1).Party B has the authority and agrees to grant Party A the rights to use, for forfaiting transaction that subjects to the CPF, and

Whereas, Party B acts as the Information Broker in forfaiting transaction.

Whereas, Party A acts as the Licensed Bank that desires to acquire the license of CPF for forfaiting transaction that subject to the CPF and the Counter party is Other Licensed Bank.

NOW THEREFORE, the Parties set forth the terms and conditions of the Contract:

一、释义

Article 1. Definitions

1.1**寰宇贸融**，指发起人贸易融资业务品牌。

Universe Trade Finance means a brand of trade finance business owned by Originator

1.2**福费廷业务**，指卖出行作为贸易融资项下未到期债权未到期债权（以下简称"相

关债权"）的唯一合法受益人或其代理人，在相关债权已由买入行认可的银行出具 / 加具了真实有效的承兑 / 保兑的情况下，将其按约定的交易价格全部或部分无追索权地转让给买入行的业务。

Forfaiting transaction means the transaction that the Grantor Bank acts as the sole legal and beneficial owner or owner's broker of outstanding payment claim(hereinafter "relevant claim") under trade finance, where the relevant claim has been issued/confirmed by a bank approved by the Purchaser Bank, should be transferred wholly or partially to the Purchaser Bank without recourse at the agreed transaction price.

1.3 **签约行**，指与发起人签约本合同且约定遵循惯例的银行，包括甲方在内。

Licensed Bank means the bank that signs the contract with the Originator and agreed to subject to the CPF,including Party A.

1.4 **工作日**，是指买卖双方所在国家或地区银行正常营业的一天。如果相关交易的支付货币与前述国家或地区的货币不同，则"工作日"也应包括支付货币所在地金融中心的银行正常营业的一天。

Business day means a day (not being a Saturday or Sunday) on which banks are open for business in the jurisdictions of both the Grantor Bank and the Purchaser Bank, and if the currency of payment concerning the relevant Transaction is different from the currency in the aforesaid jurisdictions, also infers to days on which banks are open for business in the financial center of the currency to that relevant Transaction.

1.5 **买卖双方**，指福费廷业务中的买入行和卖出行。

Trading parties mean the Grantor Bank and the Purchaser Bank in forfaiting transaction.

1.6 **人行**，指中国人民银行。

PBOC means The People's Bank Of China.

1.7 **人行支付系统**，指中国人民银行的中国国家现代化支付系统。

CNAPS means The China National Advanced Payment System produced by PBOC.

1.8 **大额支付系统**，指中国人民银行的大额实时支付子系统。

HVPS means The High Value Payment System Produced by PBOC.

1.9 **交易文件**，指在福费廷交易中的所涉及的文件和电文，包括但不限于明确引用本惯例的文件或电文，《福费廷申请书》、《债权转让书》、通过大额支付系统发送的债权转让确认电文等。

Transaction Document(s) means any document(s) or message(s) via SWIFT/HVPS in a forfaiting transaction, including but not limited to any forfaiting transaction that expressly refers to the CPF, Offer Letter, Letter of Assignment, Confirmation of Letter of Assignment via HVPS,etc.

1.10 **ISBN**，指国际标准书号。

ISBN means The International Standard Book Number.

二、总则

Article 2. General Provisions

2.1业务模式：

Business mode:

在交易文件中明示遵循惯例的签约行互为交易对手，乙方做信息中介，不做买卖双方的交易对手。乙方不经手任何交易单据。乙方不得为任何福费廷业务提供担保。乙方为甲方提供询报价、业务信息咨询等服务，乙方可在甲方同意的情况下，就单笔业务收取金融信息服务费。

The Grantor Bank and the Purchaser Bank that expressly indicate their transaction is subject to the CPF in the Transaction Documents are counterparties. Party B acts only as the information broker but not counterparty of the Grantor Bank and the Purchaser Bank,nor shall Party B handle any transaction documentation. Party B shall not guarantee for any forfaiting transaction. The services that Party B provide to Party A includes price inquiry, transaction information consultation and services likewise. Party B may charge Party A for broker service fee by transaction with the prior consent of Party A.

2.2惯例及有关交易文件是本合同不可分割的组成部分，甲乙双方及甲方之交易对手均受其条款约束。如本合同或惯例与交易文件出现任何不一致，以交易文件的规定为准，如本合同与惯例出现任何不一致，以惯例的规定为准。

The CPF and the related Transaction Documents are integral parts that make the composition to this Contract. Party A and Party B and Party A's counterparties are subject to the terms and conditions of the Contract, including The CPF and the Transaction Documents. In the event of any inconsistency exists between the Transaction Documents and the Contract or the CPF, the Transaction Documents shall prevails against the others. And in times of any inconsistency exists between the Contract and The CPF, it's the CPF that prevails.

2.3 附件 1 是本合同不可分割的组成部分。

Appendix 1 is the integral part to this Contract.

三、合同文件管理

Article 3. Legal Document Management

3.1 惯例出版发行：

The CPF Publishing and issuing:

乙方负责惯例的出版发行，确保取得全球唯一的 ISBN 编号供甲方在交易文件中引用。

Party B is responsible for publishing and issuing of the CFP, and pledging to get the unique ISBN number in the world for Party A to reference in the Transaction Documents.

3.2 本合同是确保甲方及其交易对手承认惯例法律效力的重要依据，由乙方负责与每一家签约行签署。

This Contract is the vital basis for Party A and Party A's counterparties to acknowledge legal validity of the CPF, which shall be signed by Party B with each Licensed Bank.

3.3 合同原件管理：

Management to the original version of the contract:

乙方负责保存与各签约行签订本合同的原件。任何签约行因查询、检查、仲裁、诉讼等原因，需要乙方提供其交易对手签署的本合同原件，乙方依据签约行书面申请提供，签约行应在申请中说明合理原因及借用期限。甲方同意乙方向有关交易对手提供合同正本。

Party B is responsible for keeping all the original contract signed with the Licensed Banks. If any Licensed Bank for inquiry, inspection, arbitration, litigation and other reasons, requests in which Party B to provide the original contract signed by its counterparty, Party B shall provide it according to the Licensed Bank written application, in which the Licensed Bank shall state reasonable reasons and borrowing period. Party A agrees that Party B shall provide the original contract to the relevant counterparties.

3.4 合同复印件管理：

Management to the copies of the contract:

因遵循惯例办理业务需要，甲方有权要求乙方提供交易对手与乙方签订的本合同复印件并留存备查。甲方同意乙方向有关交易对手提供本合同复印件。

For the Transaction that subject to the CPF, Party A can request Party B to provide a copy of the Contract signed by the counterparty and Party B and keep it for future reference.Party A allows Party B to provide a copy of the contract to its counterparty.

四、交易对手管理

Article 4. Counterparty management

4.1 交易对手资格：

Eligible counterparty:

与发起人签署本合同的银行即为签约行，有资格做遵循惯例办理福费廷业务的交易对手。

The bank that signs the contract with the Originator is the Licensed Bank, and will be eligible counterparty for forfaiting transaction that subject to the CPF.

4.2 交易对手身份核实：

Counterparty identity verification:

甲方可利用 SWIFT 系统、中国人民银行大额支付系统的电文及通讯资料核实交易对手身份。甲方不得与无法核实身份的交易对手交易。

Party A may verify the identity of the counterparty by message via SWIFT,HVPS and contact details. Party A shall not transact with a counterparty whose identity is unable to verify.

五、通讯管理

Article 5.Management to contact details

5.1 联系资料：

Contact details：

甲乙双方应向对方及甲方交易对手提供真实且有效的联系方式，包括电话、Email、通讯地址、人行支付系统行号（如有）、SWIFT CODE（如有）。

Both parties shall provide with authentic and effective contact details that include telephone number, email address, address, CNAPS CODE(if any) and SWIFT CODE(if any) to each other and to Party A's counterparty.

5.2 资料变更：

Change of contact details:

甲乙双方通讯资料发生变更时，应在变更发生日之前通过传真或电子邮件通知对方和所有交易对手。

Any change of the contact details should be informed to the other party and all the counterparties by fax or e-mail before the change of the contact details.

5.3 送达管理：

Delivery management:

甲乙双方每个工作日至少查收一次电子邮箱，有关邮件记录至少保存90天。甲方每工作日至少查收一次 SWIFT 和大额支付系统电文。

Both Parties shall check e-mail at least once every business day, and the mail records should be kept for at least 90 days. Party A ought to check its SWIFT(if any) and HVPS(if any) message at the frequency of at least once per business day.

5.4 失职责任：

Negligence of duty:

因下列原因给他人造成的损失，由责任方承担：

1：未及时查收邮件、电文的；

2：邮件记录丢失或被盗的；

3：电子邮箱、电话、传真、SWIFT、人行支付系统被他人使用（含丢失或被盗）的。

Whereas the following events causing damages to parties concerned, the responsible party shall bear the losses caused:

Event A: failing to check the e-mail and message in time;

Event B: mail records lost and leakage;

Event C: mail, telephone, fax, SWIFT, and bank payment system being used(lost or stolen included) by others.

六、合同终止

Article 6. Termination of contract

6.1 甲方有权通过书面文件或电子邮件通知乙方终止合同。

Party A has the right to terminate the Contract by a written or e-mail notice.

6.2 甲方有出现如下情形，乙方有权通过书面文件或电子邮件通知终止本合同：

In case of Party A engaging the following events, Party B has the right to terminate the Contract by written or e-mail notice:

（1）被吊销或注销业务经营资格；

Event 1. Party A is being revoked or have its business qualification cancelled;

（2）被吊销或注销营业执照；

Event 2. Party A is being revoked or have its business license cancelled;

（3）有重大违反法律、法规或国际惯例的行为；

Event 3. Party A has conduct serious violations to laws, regulations or international customs;

（4）信用情况严重恶化或发生重大风险事件的。

Event 4. Party A's business standing is seriously deteriorating or experiencing severe risk.

合同终止后，乙方应立即通知与甲方存在未到期业务的交易对手。

After the termination of the Contract, Party B shall notify Party A's counterparties who have undue transaction without delay.

6.3 发生如下情况时惯例终止使用：

Conditions for termination of CPF:

6.3.1 因市场环境发生重大变化，惯例主要条款已不再适用时，乙方负责通过 Email 通知所有签约行。

Party B is responsible for notifying all Licensed Banks by email when the main terms and conditions are no longer applicable due to grand changes in the market environment.

6.3.2 乙方被吊销营业执照、责令关闭或解散或乙方决定提前解散清算的。

Party B has its business license revoked or is ordered to be closed or dissolved, or Party B decides to dissolve in advance; .

6.3.3 相关法律法规或者监管、司法文书要求终止的。

Being terminated by the requirement of the relevant laws, regulations, or regulatory and judicial documents.

6.4 依据惯例办理的福费廷业务在本合同终止或惯例终止后继续有效，直至业务到期终止。

The forfaiting transaction, which is governed by the CPF will remain valid after the termination of the Contract or the CPF, until the transaction mature.

七、准据法、争议解决和主导语言

Article 7.Governing Laws,Disputes Resolution and Ruling Language

本合同以中、英文书就。如中英文版本间存在任何差异以☑中文□英文版本为准。

本合同适用☑中华人民共和国□英国□其他：＿＿＿＿＿＿法律，争议应协商解决，

无法协商的任何一方可在甲方注册地法院提起诉讼。福费廷交易的准据法、诉讼或仲裁地和主导语言可由买卖双方在交易文件中约定。

This Contract is written in Chinese and English. In case of any discrepancy between the English and Chinese version, the ☑ Chinese ☐ English version prevails. This Contract shall be governed by and construed in accordance with the laws of ☑ P.R.China ☐ England ☐ Other: _____ .

If any dispute related with this contract cannot be resolved through amicable negotiation, any party can bring such dispute to the court at the place of Party A's registered address.

The governing laws, litigation or arbitration place and ruling language of forfaiting transaction may be negotiated and stipulated in the Transaction Documents between Trading parties.

八、违约责任
Article 8.Responsibility of breachment

因当事人一方未履行本合同（包含惯例和交易文件）义务，或与第三人恶意串通，对发起人或其他交易对手造成损失的，应承担实际损失（包括可得利益损失）的赔偿责任。

If a party fails to fulfill its obligations under the Contract (including the CPF and Transaction Documents), or maliciously colludes with a third party and causes losses to the Originator or other counterparty, the misconductor shall be liable for the actual loss (including prospect interest).

九、合同效力
Article 9. Effectiveness of the contracts

9.1本合同经甲乙双方签字或盖章之日起生效，甲方没有公章的，本合同自双方签字之日起生效。

The effective date of this contract shall commence upon the date of signature or seal by parties hereto. In case of Party A have no company seal, the effective date of this contract shall commence upon the date of signature by parties hereto.

9.2本合同壹式肆份，甲乙双方各持贰份，扫描件与原件具有同等法律效力。

This contract is signed in four copies, Party A and Party B have two of each. Scanned copies hold the same legal effect as the originals.

甲方:

For and on behalf of Party A

有权签字人:

Authorized Signature:

甲方盖章 (如有):

seal of party A(if any):

日期:

Signed/Sealed this day of:

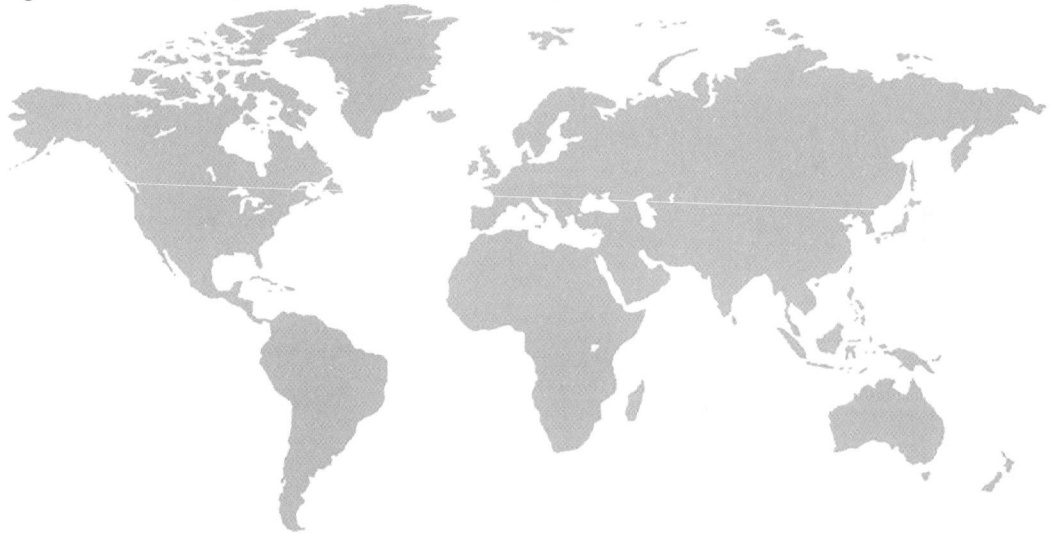

乙方:

For and on behalf of Party B

有权签字人:

Authorized Signature:

乙方盖章:

seal of party B:

日期:

Signed&Sealed this day of:

附件1： 出版物《寰宇贸融福费廷惯例3.9版》， 深圳市投友亲金融信息服务有限公司编著， 国际标准书号:978-7-5615-7173-6。

Appendix 1:publication, Universe Trade Finance Customs and Practice for Forfaiting version 3.9, compiled by Universe Trade Finance Information Service Co., Ltd., ISBN: 978-7-5615-7173-6

编写顾问组
Consultative Group
（以姓名笔划为序排名不分先后 /all names are arranged in no particular order)

主编: 史翔 深圳市投友亲金融信息服务有限公司 总经理

Chief editor:Shi Xiang General manager, Universe Trade Finance Information Service Co., Ltd.

副主编:

Associate editor:

付景璋 天津农商银行国际业务部 国际商会中国国家委员会银行委员会保理福费廷专家

Fu Jingzhang International dept, Tianjin Rural Commercial Bank; Forfaiting&Factoring Specialist, ICC China Bank Committee

李畅 恒丰银行交易银行部

Li Chang Transaction banking dept, Heng Feng Bank

王栋涛 北京银行杭州运河支行负责人 国际商会跟单结算纠纷裁决专家 国际商会中国国家委员会信用证和保函专家 浙江省银行业协会培训专家库成员

Wang Dongtao sub-branch manager,Bank of Beijing Hangzhou Yunhe sub-branch， ICC DOCDEX Expert，L/C & Demand Guarantees Expert, ICC China，Expert for training,Zhejiang Association of Bank

编写顾问:

Consultative Group Members:

马笑匀 江苏高的律师事务所 高级合伙人；中国国际经济贸易仲裁委员会 仲裁员

Sharon MA Senior Partner, G&D Law Firm; Arbitrator, CIETAC

王中华 上海锦天城（青岛）律师事务所 律师，高级合伙人，仲裁员

Wang Zhonghua Attorney-at-law&Senior Partner&Arbitrator, Allbright(Qingdao) Law Offices

刘刚 美国国泰银行北京代表处 首席代表

Leonard Liu Chief Representative, Beijing Representative Office, Cathay Bank

刘明艳 济宁银行贸易金融部 总经理

Molly General manager, Trade finance dept, Bank of Jining

刘栋 北京炜衡（上海）律师事务所 高级合伙人，涉外 / 海事 / 保险业务部主任，中英两国仲裁员

Dong LIU Shanghai office, W&H Law Firm Senior Partner & Director of International Commercial Department&arbitrator at China and UK

刘艳秀 锦州银行国际业务部 总经理

Liu Yanxiu General manager, International dept, Bank of Jinzhou

闫进波 晋商银行国际业务部

Franklyn Yan International dept, Jinshang Bank

闫晓慧 齐鲁银行公司银行部

Xiaohui Yan Corporate Banking dept, Qilu Bank

汤志贤 中国工商银行首尔分行贸易融资部主管

Tang Zhixian Director, Trade finance dept, ICBC Seoul branch

许伟 莱商银行贸易金融部

Xu Wei Trade finance dept, Lai Shang Bank

苏志成 美国国际银行法律与实务学院 副董事

Soh Chee Seng Associate Director, Institute of International Banking Law & Practice, Inc., USA

杨云帆 四川天府银行国际业务中心 副总经理

Yang Yunfan Deputy general manager, International business center, Sichuan Tianfu Bank

吴志毅 厦门银行贸易金融部 产品经理

Wu Zhiyi product manager, Trade finance dept, Xiamen Bank

何贤君 北京银行杭州分行国际业务部

He Xianjun International dept, Bank of Beijing Hangzhou branch

张洪涛 北京大成（青岛）律师事务所 合伙人

Michael Zhang partner, Dentons(Qingdao) Law Offices

张超 柳州银行贸易金融部 单证中心经理

Zhang Chao Documentation Center Manager, Trade Financing Dept, Bank of Liuzhou

陈惠莉 成都农商银行国际业务部 副总经理

Huili Chen Deputy general manager, International dept, Chengdu Rural Commercial Bank

范利军

Frank

林雨晴 安徽禹风律师事务所

Lynn Yuki YuFeng Law Firm, BengBu, Anhui Province

呼勖光 山东龙口农村商业银行国际业务部 总经理

Hu Xunguang General manager, International dept, Longkou Rural Commercial Bank,Shandong Province, China

罗伊程 巴基斯坦哈比银行乌鲁木齐分行贸易融资及同业部 总经理

Luo Yicheng Head of Trade finance&FI dept, Habib bank(Pakistan) Urumqi branch

周剑玫 营口沿海银行国际业务部 总经理

Zhou Jianmei General manager, International dept, Yingkou Coastal Bank

周彩莲 浙江温州龙湾农村商业银行国际业务部 总经理

Zhou Cailian International dept, Longwan Rural Commercial Bank, WenZhou city, Zhejiang Province, China

郑致华 文莱伊斯兰银行新加坡代表处 首席代表

Klaus Tay Head, Singapore Representative Office, Bank Islam Brunei Darussalam

钟梅云 巴基斯坦联合银行阿联酋分行金融机构部 客户经理

Meiyun Zhong Relationship Manager, FI dept, United Bank(Pakistan) UAE branch

顾荣 江苏泰兴农村商业银行国际业务部 总经理

Gu Rong General manager, Head of international dept, Taixing Rural Commercial Bank,Jiangsu Province, China

郭超 绵阳市商业银行国际业务部 产品经理

Guo Chao Product manager, International dept, Mianyang City Commercial Bank

萨哈尔·穆罕默德·菲克里 埃及联合国民银行金融机构部 高级副总裁

Sahar Mohamed Fikry SVP, FI Division Head, Union National Bank,Egypt

曹丽霞 东营银行股份有限公司国际业务部 总经理

Cao Lixia General manager, international dept, Dongying Bank Co., Ltd.

梁华 烟台银行贸易金融中心 产品经理

Katherine Leung Product manager, Trade finance centre, Yantai bank

董昭材 中国银行新加坡分行福费廷中心 主管

Tang Zhao Cai Director, Forfaiting unit, Bank of China Singapore Branch

蒋俊 中国农业银行香港分行贸易融资部 团队负责人

Jiang Jun Team leader, Trade finance dept, Agricultural Bank of China Hongkong branch

谢赫·穆哈马德·夏立克 巴基斯坦国民银行北京代表处 首席代表

Shaikh Muhammad Shariq chief representative, National Bank of Pakistan, Representative Office, Beijing, China

赵鹏 巴基斯坦国民银行北京代表处 首席代表助理

Peter Zhao Assistant to chief representative, National Bank of Pakistan, Representative Office, Beijing, China

楼雨燕 江苏姜堰农村商业银行有限公司国际业务部 总经理

Yuyan Lou General manager, International dept, Jiangyan Rural Commercial Bank Co., Ltd., Jiangsu Province, China

部分法律顾问简历 /Resume of some legal advisors:

教育背景
- 澳大利亚新南威尔士大学法学硕士（公司法 / 商法）
- 南京大学金融总裁班（金融培训）

Education & Trainings
- LLM on Corporate Law / Business Law of University of New South Wales, Australia.
- CEO Class of Finance（Finance training course）, Nanjing University

业务专长
- 公司投资与并购
- 国际贸易
- 银行与融资
- 私募基金与资本市场

Specialties
- Corporate Investment and Merger & Acquisitions
- International Trade
- Banking and Financing
- Private Equity Funds and Capital markets

社会职务
- 中国国际经济贸易仲裁委员会仲裁员
- 中国国际贸易促进委员会 / 中国国际商会调解中心调解员
- 江苏省国际商会副会长
- 江苏省国际商事法律服务中心调解员
- 南京市进出口商会副会长
- 南京市公共外交协会常务理事
- 南京 / 青岛 / 宁波仲裁委员会仲裁员
- 上市公司独立董事

马笑匀 /Sharon MA
高级合伙人 涉外业务部主任
Senior Partner & Director of International Commercial Department
Email：ma__xiaoyun6@hotmail.com
电话 /Telephone：+86 (25) 8473 1776
传真 /Fax：+86 (25) 8470 3306
手机 /Mobile：+86 158 0515 8000
地址： 中国南京市汉中路169号金丝利国际大厦12层
邮编：210029
Address: 12F Kingsley Towers,169 Hanzhong Road, Nanjing, 210029, China

Affiliates
- Arbitrator of China International Economic and Trade Arbitration

Commission

- Mediator of China Council for the Promotion of International Trade / China International Chamber of Commerce Mediation Center
- Vice president of Jiangsu International Chamber of Commerce
- Mediator of Jiangsu International Commercial Legal Service Center
- Vice president of Nanjing import and Export Chamber of Commerce
- Executive Director of Nanjing Public Diplomacy Association
- Arbitrator of Nanjing / Qingdao / Ningbo Arbitration Commission
- Independent Directors of listed companies

奖项荣誉

- 中华全国律协涉外律师"领军人才"
- 中华全国律协"一带一路"项目跨境律师人才库律师
- 江苏省十佳涉外律师
- 江苏企业国际化专家库专家
- 江苏省"一带一路"法律服务研究中心研究员
- 珠海市"一带一路"法律服务专家库专家
- 第二届夏季青年奥林匹克运动会法律事务工作特别感谢奖

Awards

- International Legal Professionals from All China Lawyers Association

- *Lawyer of International Lawyers Pool* for "the Belt and Road" projects from All China Lawyers Association
- *The Top Ten International Lawyers of Jiangsu Province*
- Expert in the International Experts Pool of Jiangsu Enterprises
- Researcher of Jiangsu "the Belt and Road" Legal Services Research Center
- Expert of Zhuhai "the Belt and Road" Legal Services Experts Pool
- *Special Thanks Award* of the legal affairs of the second summer Youth Olympic Games

业绩经历

马笑匀律师长期为南京银行、江苏省盐业集团、苏美达集团、江苏省海外合作投资公司、金拱门（中国）、沙索（中国）、塔塔（中国）等知名企业、上市公司提供优质、高效的法律服务，涉及的行业包括工业及智能制造、新能源与环保、医疗健康与生物医药、银行与私募基金等。

马律师擅长境内外投资与并购，经手的确成硅化法国马赛投资项目系中法两国邦交重点项目，中阿产能合作示范园及金融平台项目系国家发改委"一带一路"重点项目，锡南铸机竞购意大利 IMF 资产项目获得江苏省十佳涉外法律服务案例奖，剑桥大学-南京市江北新区国际健康城合作项目为央视新闻联播所报道。

马律师曾作为"一带一路"沿线国家

法律环境国别报告协调与撰稿人，并多次受国家发改委国际合作中心、江苏省商务厅、浙江省财政厅等机构的邀请进行授课。

Experience

For a long time, Ms Ma has provided high-quality and efficient legal services to a lot of well-known enterprises and listed companies such as Bank of Nanjing, SUYAN Group, SUMEC Group Corporation, JOCIC, Golden Arches (China), Sasol (China) and Tata (China), etc. Her clients are involved in different industries such as Industrial and Intelligent Manufacturing, New Energy and Environmental Protection, Medical Health and Biomedicine, Banking and Private Equity Fund, etc.

Ms Ma specializes in domestic and foreign investment and mergers and acquisitions cases she has represented clients and leaded many overseas investment projects, including the investment project in Marseilles of France from Quecheng Silicon Chemical Co., Ltd., which is one of the key projects of diplomatic relations between China and France; China-U.A.E. Industrial Cooperation Demonstration Zone project is one of the National Development and Reform Commission "the Belt and Road" key projects; the project of acquiring Italy IMF assets representing Wuxi Xinan Foundry Machinery Co., Ltd. has won *the award of the top ten foreign law service cases in Jiangsu*; University of Cambridge - Nanjing Jiangbei New District International Health City cooperation project was reported by CCTV news.

Ms Ma has worked as the coordinator and writer of the country reports on national legal environment of those countries along "the Belt and Road". She has been invited many times to give lectures by different institutions such as National Development and Reform Commission International Cooperation Center, the Department of Commerce of Jiangsu Province and the Department of Finance of Zhejiang Province.

教育与培训

● 大连海事大学博士研究生（海商法）

● 英国伦敦大学法学硕士（国际商法）

● 中国政法大学法学学士（国际经济法）

● 最高人民法院派遣先后在英国高等法院商事法庭、Clyde & Co. 律所、7 King's Bench Walk 律所实习，并赴联合国国际海事组织、英国议会、最高法院、监狱等机构考察调研

● 最高人民法院派遣中海集团进行航海理论培训和国际远洋货轮驾驶实践

Education & Trainings

● PhD Candidate on Maritime Law of Dalian Maritime University

● LLM on International & Comparative Commercial Law of London University, SOAS

● LLM on Maritime Law of Dalian Maritime University

● LLB of China University of Political Science and Law

● Internship in the Commercial Court of High Court, Clyde & Co. London Office,Barrister Chambers of 7 King's Bench Walk, organized by the :Supreme People's Court PRC

● Trainings of navigation practical skills on an ocean ship for several months, organized by the Supreme People's Court PRC

刘 栋 /Dong LIU

北京炜衡（上海）律师事务所

Shanghai office,W&H Law Firm

高级合伙人 涉外 / 海事 / 保险业务部主任

Senior Partner & Director of International Commercial Department

Email: liudong@wh-law.com

liu.dong@vip.163.com

电话 /Telephone：+86 (21) 2225 7655

总机 /Direct：+86 (21) 2225 7666

传真 /Fax：+86 (21) 2225 7667

手机 /Mobile：+86 186 2175 5333

地址：中国上海市长宁区华山路 1368 号

邮编：200052

Address: No. 1368 Huashan Road, Changning District, Shanghai, 200052, China

社会职务

● 英国特许仲裁员协会中级会员

(MCIArb)

- 中国海事仲裁委员会 (CMAC)、伦敦海事仲裁员协会 (LMAA) 仲裁员
- 广州、青岛、宁波仲裁委员会仲裁员
- 中国国际贸易促进委员会 / 中国国际商会调解员 & 投资争端调解员
- 英国广州总领事馆中国法高级专家顾问
- 上海海事大学法学院客座教授
- 华东师范大学法律硕士兼职导师
- 上海市律协国际贸易专业委员会委员

Affiliates

- MCIArb (Member of Chartered Institute of Arbitrators)
- Arbitrator at LMAA (London Maritime Arbitrators Association) and CMAC (China Maritime Arbitration Commission)
- Mediator at ICC China / CCOIC / CCPIT
- Arbitrator at Guangzhou / Qingdao / Ningbo Arbitration Commission
- Senior Expert Advisor of Chinese Law for British Consulate General
- Guest Professor at Shanghai Maritime University
- LLM Supervisor (Part-time) at East China Normal University

工作语言

- 中文
- 英文

Working language

- Chinese
- English

业务专长

- 跨境争议解决
- 国际贸易与融资
- 海事海商
- 保险

Specialties

- Arbitration & Litigation
- International Trade & Finance
- Shipping
- Insurance

工作经历

1997年7月至2011年7月就职于大连海事法院，历任书记员、助理审判员、审判员，并曾兼任审委会秘书、团委书记等职务。在多年的审判工作中，审理过数千件各类海事、商事案件，包括多件在国内国际具有较大影响的疑难案件。因审判业绩突出，曾被授予"最佳法官"荣誉称号。

2011年8月起加入在涉外商事、航运和保险等领域连续多年被国际各评级机构评为顶级的某律师事务所，任职高级顾问，为多件由最高法院、高级法院审理的重大疑难案件制定诉讼策略。

2013年初加入北京炜衡（上海）律师事务所，任职高级合伙人，并担任炜衡集团的涉外民商事法律业务负责人；曾多次作为中国法律专家，为加拿大、日本等国的法庭、仲裁庭提供法律专家意见书；其律师团队曾被评为上海长宁区"法律服务领

先专业团队"。

Experience

Mr. Liu was a senior judge in the Maritime Court for more than ten years. During that period he heard thousands of cases including some hard cases well known by shipping and insurance communities in and out of China. He was ever honored as "the Best Judge" of the court.

Mr. Liu left the court in 2011 and became a senior consultant in a Chinese leading law firm in international commercial, shipping and insurance areas. He led making litigation strategies for important lawsuits being submitted to the Supreme People's Court and some Higher People's Courts.

Mr. Liu initiated a new career as senior partner with W&H Law Firm since 2013 and has been in charge of International Commercial Department. He was invited as the expert witness of Chinese law for several arbitrations and litigations in Canada, Japan and the UK and his legal opinions were well adopted by the tribunals.His team was honored as Leading Professional Legal Team of Shanghai Changning District.

深圳市投友亲金融信息服务有限公司
Universe Trade Finance Information Service Co., Ltd.
网站 /Website:www.forfaiting.ltd; www.forfaiting.shop

发起人简介

Originator Profile

深圳市投友亲金融信息服务有限公司 (以下简称本公司) 成立于2015年11月，是贸易融资业务的金融信息服务商。本公司建有包括网站、微信小程序、公众号等多渠道的贸易融资业务信息平台，为全球金融机构提供询报价和业务信息咨询服务，标的产品主要有国内及国际信用证买断式转贴现、保理二级市场、同业代付、融资性保函等业务。

Universe Trade Finance Information Service Co., Ltd.(referred to as our company hereafter), which was founded in November 2015, is an interbank information broker for trade finance. Our company has a trade financing information system, including website, WeChat Mini apps, linkedin group and other channels to provide inquiry pricing and advisory services for financial institutions.The target products of inquiry pricing and advisory services include Forfaiting under L/C, Re-Factoring, Interbank Financing and Payment, Financing guarantee/SBLC,etc.

机构客户包括国有大行、股份制、城商、农商、外资银行和在海外的法人银行。用户群体已达6300多人，在五大洲均有分布，以华人银行为主 (含中国、新加坡、马来西亚)。本公司业务量维持在千亿人民币 / 年的水平，在中国福费廷市场上有较大影响力。

Institutional customers include all tiers Chinese banks and overseas corporate banks. Our user base is over more than 6300 and is distributed all over the world. They are mainly based on Chinese banks (including China,Singapore, Malaysia). Our business scale is maintained at the level of equivalent CNY 100 billion per year and has grent influence in Chinese forfaiting market.

本公司网站 /Our Website：www.forfaiting.ltd; www.forfaiting.shop

领英群 /linkedin group:https://www.linkedin.com/groups/10378002

微信公众号 /WeChat Official accounts	微信小程序 /WeChat Mini apps
Scan our QR code using wechat	微信扫一扫，使用小程序 Scan our QR code using wechat